The Little Library Year

Kate Young is an award-winning food writer, cook and bookworm. Her first book, *The Little Library Cookbook*, was shortlisted for the Fortnum & Mason Debut Food Book Award, and won a World Gourmand food writing award. She was named Blogger of the Year in 2017 by the Guild of Food Writers. To find out more, visit her blog (thelittlelibrarycafe.com), or follow her (@bakingfiction) on Twitter and Instagram.

Lean Timms is a freelance travel, food and lifestyle photographer. Although born in Australia, Lean has been lucky enough to photograph for editorials and publications throughout the world. She is based in Canberra, Australia.

The
Little
Library
Year

Recipes and reading
to suit each season

KATE YOUNG

An Anima Book

First published in 2019 by Head of Zeus Ltd

Copyright © Kate Young, 2019
Photography © Lean Timms, 2019

1 3 5 7 9 10 8 6 4 2

A catalogue record for this book is available from
the British Library.

ISBN
9781788545280 { HB }
9781788545297 { E }

Design by Jessie Price
Photography by Lean Timms

Printed in Serbia by Publikum

Head of Zeus Ltd
5–8 Hardwick Street
London EC1R 4RG
www.headofzeus.com

For Ingela,
for the advice about Pepparkakor,
for your always perfect elderflower cordial,
and for giving me a home when I needed one most.

Contents

Introduction

I arrived in England on a grey March day in 2009. The Underground journey from Heathrow to Mile End took me through the western boroughs of London: tiled roofs and chimney pots in neat rows and the clouds as dark as oyster shells, rain falling from them in a barely perceptible mist. The city was exactly as I had expected to find it. Over the next weeks, daffodils bloomed, people started shedding their heavy coats, and my walk to work became greener by the day. Spring was arriving.

Right from those early days, my love of living in England became knitted to my love of the seasons, to discovering a place where there is a right time for a bowl of soup and a re-read of *Jane Eyre*, and also a right time for snacking on radishes and pulling *Brideshead Revisited* down from the shelf. I'm forever told (by those with longer memories than mine) that the seasons are not as distinct as they once were, but they are certainly more defined than the 'hot and wet' and 'a bit less hot and less wet' that I grew up with in Brisbane. Throughout my first year here – gloriously bright and beautiful spring, the blisteringly hot and heavy summer, the night that the leaves started to fall from the trees – I found it impossible not to be changed by the seasons.

I revisited books that felt appropriately cosy, or ones where you could almost feel the heat radiating off the page. I explored the greengrocer, and started to pay greater attention to the arrival of key ingredients; favourite fruits and vegetables that I would, in later years, anticipate in earnest. I walked through markets in search of apple varieties I had never tasted, set weekends aside for elderflower or blackberry picking, and mourned the loss of the thin green asparagus spears that came with the arrival of summer. I grew up comfortable in the kitchen, but it was in England that I became a cook, hunting for ways to capture and honour the shifting seasons.

That first year in England, the seasons waxed and waned until, inevitably, March arrived again. I found myself looking forward to the end of winter, those bleak grey months at the start of the year, as much as I had the spring, autumn and summer. I remember standing on a train platform with two friends, hoods pulled up, and eyes shielded, declaring my adoration for drizzling rain. The way I see it, it's all part and parcel of the same: the long sunny evenings, the crisp winter mornings, the dreary March days. They're each so wonderful precisely because of their entirely transient nature, because of the way they flow into each other, because they are each – in their own way – worth embracing and celebrating while we have them.

Regardless of my love for food, my life is not spent in a farmer's market, and there are days when I cook with whatever I have to hand, where 'seasonal cooking' is as much about seeking out comfort and warmth as it is hunting for a specific ingredient. Our food supply chain has altered so enormously in the past decades that it is possible, should you wish, to lay your hands on strawberries in March, and find asparagus in October. And so, in this book, I wanted to share recipes that are as much about a seasonal mood as they are ingredients: meals for one in January, when hibernation is practically a necessity; food that can be easily flung into a picnic basket in late spring; canapés and a cocktail for the inevitable parties in the lead-up to Christmas.

I have broken the year down into six parts: those **Long winter nights** in January and February, the **First signs of spring** in March and April, the green months of May and June, when there is **Spring in abundance**, the **Height of summer** in July and August, the weeks **When the leaves start to turn** in September and October, and the final months of the year, **As the days grow short**. From year to year, depending on the weather, and on where you are in the world, these seasons will shift and change. But I wanted to acknowledge the distinction between each season; that the last part of the year, those bright, twinkly winter weeks, is entirely different from the grey months after New Year. And that those first moments of spring are nothing like the warmer days in May, before summer arrives in earnest.

In short, I have written *The Little Library Year* as a literary and culinary almanac, a celebration of each and every season, and a way to capture the year in books, and in food. I hope that it takes you, whether reader or cook (or both), from January to December – this year, and in the years to come. Happy reading, and happy eating.

Notes on reading

It was a particularly balmy June day when I first picked up a copy of *Anna Karenina* in a charity shop. I carried it with me on my daily commute, crawling through it a couple of pages at a time, struggling to find purchase with the story while on a sweaty London Tube. I was only a hundred pages in when I abandoned it. Six months later, in the depths of winter in my freezing-cold flat, I pulled it back down from the shelf, and took it with me into the bath. This time I devoured it. The next day, back on the train again, I lost myself in the detailed characters, and in the epic scope – I was so distracted that I missed my stop. I flew through the book in little more than a week.

The experience reinforced my long-held belief that there is a 'right' time for every book on my shelf. It makes sense to revisit Cassandra Mortmain's world in *I Capture the Castle* in late spring, and to join Harry, Hermione, and Ron on the train back to Hogwarts in early September. At Christmas, I read Charles Dickens, and Louisa May Alcott, and Noel Streatfeild, revelling in descriptions of houses dressed for the season, and abundant holiday meals. In the hottest summer months I want to be with talented Tom Ripley, with Gerald Durrell's family (and their animals), and with Ferrante's Lila and Elena, dipping a toe into the Mediterranean. And when it's cold and bleak outside in January, I return to Narnia, to the snow-filled Russian epics, and to the strange comfort of murder mysteries, read by the fire.

The books in the pages that follow are some of my very favourites, ones I continue to return to, and find myself frequently recommending to friends. In each of them I have felt a tangible connection with a particular season, a holiday, or an annual event; I hope they provide you with similar atmosphere, insight, and inspiration.

Notes on recipes

The recipes in this book track the seasons, capturing elements that inspire me at different points throughout the year. There are recipes that are brought to life from the pages of my favourite novels, as well as dishes influenced by a mood, an event, or an ingredient. They reflect the way I cook: plenty of vegetables, lots of fruit, a bit of meat and a bit more fish, bread frequently employed to mop up sauces or pile things on top of, and some cakes and ice creams generous enough to share.

The food borrows from various cultures, includes two Christmas menus (one Australian and one Scandinavian), and will provide some ideas and inspiration whether you're cooking for one or for many. In my kitchen, cooking often needs to be done quickly, with ingredients that are easily accessible, and so recipes that demand your time and attention, for long evenings, or cosy weekends, are set alongside those that can be pulled together in a half-hour.

I know that a long list of required equipment may be off-putting, and so (where possible) I have made it clear when I think you really need something specific: a cake tin, some ramekins, a sheet of fine muslin for straining. But otherwise do feel free to cut out biscuits using the rim of a glass, roll out pasta using a rolling pin or wine bottle, or fill pastry for blind baking with rice. I'm a home cook, and I assume you are too – using whatever you have in your kitchen is absolutely fine.

Unless otherwise stated, I have used salted butter, whole milk, flaky sea salt, and large eggs. I have listed oven temperatures as fan and in gas mark. If you have a conventional (non-fan) oven, you'll need to increase temperatures by 20C/50F/2 gas marks.

Most of the ingredients called for are ones I hope you can find in your supermarket, or buy from your butcher, fishmonger, or greengrocer. However, if you can't find something and wish to give a recipe a try, there are a number of online supermarkets that deliver, or Google should throw up an alternative you can substitute.

Ingredients to look out for

The long winter nights
Apples, blood oranges, Brussels sprouts, cabbage, cauliflower, celeriac/celery root, celery, clementines, chicory/endive, forced rhubarb, grapefruit, horseradish, Jerusalem artichokes, kale, leeks, lemons, parsnip, pears, purple sprouting broccoli, radicchio, swede/rutabaga, sweet potato

The first signs of spring
Brussels sprouts, cauliflower, celeriac/celery root, grapefruit, purple sprouting broccoli, rhubarb, rocket/arugula, sorrel, spinach, spring greens, spring onions/scallions, watercress, wild garlic

Spring in abundance
Asparagus, broad/fava beans, elderflower, French beans, globe artichokes, gooseberries, lettuce, new potatoes, peas, radish, rhubarb, rocket/arugula, sorrel, spinach, spring greens, spring onions/scallions, strawberries, tomatoes, watercress

The height of summer
Apricots, aubergine/eggplant, basil, blackcurrants, broad/fava beans, broccoli, carrots, cherries, courgette/zucchini, fennel, French beans, globe artichokes, gooseberries, lettuce, mangetout/snow peas, nectarines, peaches, peas, peppers/bell peppers, radish, raspberries, redcurrants, rocket/arugula, spinach, strawberries, sweetcorn, Swiss chard, tomatoes, watercress, watermelon

When the leaves start to turn
Apples, aubergine/eggplant, beetroot/beets, blackberries, broccoli, cavolo nero, celeriac/celery root, celery, courgette/zucchini, damsons, elderberries, figs, globe artichokes, kale, lettuce, marrow, medlars, mushrooms, pears, plums, pumpkin, quince, radish sloes, squash, sweetcorn, Swiss chard

Baking sheet
Chopping knife and
board
Cooling rack
Fork, knife, and spoon
Frying pan/skillet
Parchment paper,
plastic wrap, and
aluminium foil
Kitchen paper towel
Large and small
saucepans/pots
Measuring jug/pitcher
Mixing bowls
Sieve/strainer
Spatula
Tea towel/dish towel
Vegetable peeler
Whisk
Wooden spoon

As the days grow short
Apples, beetroot/beets, Brussels sprouts, cavolo nero, celeriac/
celery root, chestnuts, clementines, cranberries, horseradish,
Jerusalem artichokes, kale, mushrooms, parsnips, pears, pumpkin,
quince, sloes, sweet potato, Swiss chard

Introduction

The long winter nights

The long winter nights

Nothing can be as peaceful and endless as a long winter darkness,
going on and on, like living in a tunnel where the dark sometimes
deepens into night and sometimes eases to twilight, you're screened
from everything, protected, even more alone than usual.
The True Deceiver, Tove Jansson (translated by Thomas Teal)

I love winter. I love bowls of slightly salty porridge with a spoonful of
treacle first thing in the morning, before the sun is properly in the sky.
I love the darkness, and the cold. I love roaring fires, and coats and
boots. I love sitting too close to the radiator, a book balanced on my
knees. I love roasts, and deep dishes of creamy potatoes, and generous
slices of cake beside pots of coffee. I love warming my hands around
a steaming mug of tea. I love inviting groups of friends around and
spending a day in front of good films, bringing dishes out of the oven
with reassuring regularity.

I look forward to this season every year; the long, quiet weeks
following Christmas when everyone is reluctant to leave their homes,
when I can decompress and start the year afresh. I spend much of
winter in happy hibernation, embracing my more natural introverted
state after a December spent being social. The solitude and quiet
allows me time and space to luxuriate in literature; winter is the season
during which I read most prolifically. I take frequently to my bath,
filling it with bubbles and spending hours topping up the hot water,
devouring books in their entirety. I snuggle up with woollen blankets in
my armchair, spending time with books I might not commit to at other
points in the year. Januarys past have seen me dive straight into *Anna
Karenina*, *Moby Dick*, and *A Suitable Boy*: weighty tomes that defy
the daily commute, and are best read on the sofa. I immerse myself in
worlds white with winter: in Narnia, Scandinavia, rural Russia, and the
coldest English days, when the crisp, fresh snow underfoot seems to
make its way off the page and into my living room.

At this time of year, everything happens slowly – the oven takes
longer to warm up, bread takes an age to rise, and mornings seem to
arrive at a snail's pace. It is antithetical to the way I live during the rest

of the year, when I bustle from task to task and place to place with a 'To Do' list as long as my arm. This side of Christmas, it's impossible to bustle. Even the kettle takes more time to boil.

In the deep midwinter, it often seems as if the cold will continue in perpetuity. I may love winter but, after the barren months, when much of our fresh food is pulled from beneath the ground, I begin to happily anticipate the early green shoots that herald the arrival of spring.

A cold, grey start

'You're at Ferndean, Miss Next,' replied Mary soothingly, 'one of
Mr Rochester's other properties. You will be weak; I'll bring some broth.'
I grabbed her arm.
'And Mr Rochester?'
She paused and smiled at me, patted my hand and said she would fetch
the broth.
The Eyre Affair, Jasper Fforde

Those first days after New Year, as Epiphany approaches, have an
air of strangeness about them. The world still glitters with tinsel
and decorations, department stores still push their leftover stock
– all around us, life hasn't quite returned to normal. And yet, after
the last slice of Christmas cake has been eaten, puzzles have been
broken down and put back in their boxes, and the inevitability
of returning to work lies around the corner, we are thrust into
the cold reality of January. This side of Christmas, winter is cold
and bleak.

Back home in my own kitchen, after a week or so in someone
else's, I crave warmth and comfort, but not the rich luxury of
Christmas. And so, in an attempt to stave off an unwelcome winter
cold, I make broth. I know its magic is mostly a placebo, but if it
helps *Little Women*'s Beth (though not, obviously, in the long-run),
or *Sense and Sensibility*'s Marianne, I like to believe that it can
also help me. When Thursday Next, the Swindon-based literary
detective in Jasper Fforde's *The Eyre Affair*, is injured during her
travels into the pages of *Jane Eyre* in order to rescue Jane from an
evil mastermind – I know, stay with me here – she is fed broth to
recover. It's exactly what I'd hope for if I, too, found myself in the
pages of a Victorian novel.

And so, as January begins again, I reshelve my favourite Christmas
stories, and revisit *Jane Eyre* and the grouchy Mr Rochester – both
in the original, and in Jasper Fforde's love letter to it. Their world
is bleak and grey, the food is unappetizing, and any sense of hope
comes in small doses – but it is still there. Whether you love winter
or spend it longing for spring, it's worth remembering that the
daffodils are just around the corner.

Winter broth

Broth is the ideal post-Christmas dish. The carcass from a roasted bird, broken down and stripped clean of its meat, can be kept in a box in the freezer until you need it. I'm always keen to get the most out of any meat I bring into the kitchen, and so a roast chicken will always end up as a pot of chicken stock simmering away on the hob. The addition of pearl barley and a handful of fresh herbs transforms it into a comforting supper.

Serves 4

1. Roughly chop the turnip, onion, and celery. Layer in the bottom of a saucepan along with the herbs. Place the chicken carcass or wings on top, and cover with 2 litres/8¾ cups of cold water.

2. Bring to the boil, then reduce the heat and simmer gently. Place the lid half-on. You don't want all the water to evaporate, so take a peek every now and then to ensure it's not boiling too fast. Leave it simmering away for a couple of hours, and settle in with a book.

3. Strain the broth through a sheet of muslin into a bowl, peel any final scraps of meat from the bones (you can add it to the broth later), then discard them along with the boiled vegetables, and herbs. Allow the broth to cool, then skim the top to remove any fat.

4. Pour the stock back into the washed-out saucepan, bring to the boil, and tip in the pearl barley. Put the lid back on and simmer for 40 minutes until the barley is tender. Turn off the heat, add the parsley, any last scraps of chicken, and a generous pinch of salt. Stir, taste, and serve.

1 turnip
1 onion
2 stalks celery
6 sprigs thyme
2 bay leaves
10 peppercorns
1 chicken carcass, stripped of any chunks of meat (or 200g/7oz chicken wings)
150g/heaped ¾ cup pearl barley
30g/1¼ cups finely chopped parsley
A pinch of salt

EQUIPMENT
A piece of muslin/ cheesecloth, or a very fine sieve

Cooking for one

No one who cooks, cooks alone. Even at her most solitary, a cook in the kitchen is surrounded by generations of cooks past, the advice and menus of cooks present, the wisdom of cookbook writers.
Laurie Colwin

I fear that eating alone gets a bad rap in literature. Miss Havisham and her rotting wedding cake, Barbara's lonely evenings at home in *Notes on a Scandal*, Mildred's depressingly tasteless lunches in *Excellent Women*: characters eating alone (particularly female ones) are often presented as tragic figures. But there are exceptions. I've long been inspired by Detective Montalbano's enjoyment of a late-night walk or swim followed by a glorious meal left out by his housekeeper. And though she's not always happy to be on her own, *Heartburn*'s Rachel Samstat is an expert in delicious meals for one.

Though I make my living as a cook and have never yet lived on my own, I most often find myself cooking for one. It's a ritual in which I find particular joy. When I cook, I do so with Colwin's 'generations of cooks'; inspired and encouraged by voices of writers, characters, and people I know and love. Jane Grigson gives me advice on what to do with a glut of plums. My granny nudges my hand to ensure I add the extra chilli. My dad lets me know when the barbeque is ready for a steak. Julia Child reassures me that a split hollandaise can be saved. Han Kang, in her novel *The Vegetarian*, introduces me to yuk hwe, 'a kind of beef tartare'. Every act in the kitchen – every chop, or stir, or blitz – is one that someone else has done before. Standing alone at my hob, I'm merely continuing a conversation that others have already begun.

When I am at home alone, as I make sure I am in the weeks following Christmas, I have only my mood and appetite to satisfy. Some days, a tin of beans, with hot sauce and cheese stirred through, provides exactly this. On other days, I relish the chance to use ingredients I couldn't afford, or techniques I wouldn't bother with, if I were making more than one serving. Either way, there is endless joy to be found in a meal made for one.

Yuk hwe

This Korean take on the classic beef tartare has quickly become my dream version of the dish. It isn't time consuming (there's no cooking involved) but dicing the meat perfectly will take a little effort, and it's worth buying the best beef you can get your hands on. Talk to your butcher about what might work; you need a cut that's very lean and tender.

Serves 1

1. Store the beef in the coldest part of your fridge, or pop it in the freezer for an hour before you intend to eat. It will be easier to slice this way.

2. Peel the pear and slice it into fine matchsticks. Fill a mixing bowl with iced water and drop in the sliced pear. This will prevent the pear going brown, and also ensure it's cool and crisp when you come to serving.

3. Put the soy sauce, sesame oil, honey, sesame seeds, spring onion, garlic and a generous grinding of pepper into a small bowl and mix together with a fork.

4. Now slice the beef. Start by laying the meat flat on the chopping board, and cut into 3mm/⅛in thick slices. Lay the slices flat on the board, and cut each into 3mm/⅛in strips. Finally, dice the strips into small cubes.

5. Mix the dressing through the beef. Fill a small bowl with the mixture, packing it down tightly as if it were a mould. Place in the freezer for 5 minutes to chill thoroughly. Meanwhile, drain the pear and assemble in a pile on a plate. Drop the chilled beef on top, then make an indent and place the raw egg yolk into it.

125g/4½oz raw beef
½ pear (a Korean or Nashi pear is ideal, but any nice, firm one will work)
2tsp soy sauce
2tsp sesame oil
1tsp honey
1tbsp sesame seeds
1 spring onion/scallion, very finely diced
2 cloves garlic, finely minced
Black pepper
1 egg yolk

Mussels with vermouth and fennel

After long days in an office, I have (more than once) excused myself from post-work drinks after the first pint in order to return home alone via the supermarket fish counter. Once back in the kitchen, dinner could be ready in a matter of minutes; the glistening black shells of the mussels making a comforting clatter as I carried them to the table. These are to be eaten straight from the pan, using only your hands and chunks of bread as utensils.

Serves 1

1. Rinse your mussels under cold running water. If the shells are a bit dirty, or covered in barnacles, give them a scrub. Pull any beards out by grasping them firmly and pulling in the direction of the hinge. If any of the mussels have cracked shells, or remain open after you squeeze them closed a couple of times, discard them.

2. Warm the butter over a low heat, in a lidded saucepan big enough to hold all the mussels. Soften the shallot for a couple of minutes, and then add the fennel and garlic. Fry for 5 minutes until the fennel and shallot are translucent, and your kitchen smells delicious. Keep everything moving so that the garlic doesn't burn.

3. Tip in the mussels, and stir them through the shallots and fennel. Add the vermouth, then clamp the lid down. Turn up the heat a little. Leave the mussels to steam in the pan, resisting the urge to peek for a couple of minutes. Once they've opened, stir in the cream. Chop the herbs, and sprinkle them over the top. Serve with plenty of really good bread to mop up the juices.

250g/9oz mussels
1tsp butter
1 shallot, finely sliced
Small bulb fennel, finely sliced
2 cloves garlic, finely chopped
100ml/scant ½ cup vermouth
1tbsp double/heavy cream
4 sprigs parsley
4 stalks dill

Gnocchi with Gorgonzola, walnuts, and sage

GNOCCHI
150g/5½oz floury
potatoes (Maris Pipers
are good here)
1 egg yolk
1tsp salt
30–40g/3⅔–4¾tbsp
plain/all-purpose flour

SAUCE
4 walnuts
1tsp olive oil
10 sage leaves
50g/1¾oz Gorgonzola
40ml/2½tbsp double/
heavy cream
Black pepper

EQUIPMENT
Potato ricer or fine
cheese grater

Having first made gnocchi by hand for a large dinner party, I wholeheartedly recommend that you start out by making it for one. A small batch is much more manageable, and making it in a calm kitchen with the radio for company is extraordinarily therapeutic. Try to work the dough as little as possible – if you build up the gluten you risk the gnocchi becoming tough and chewy.

Serves 1

1. Boil the potatoes (in their skins) for 25 minutes. Don't boil them too fiercely or skewer them too often, as you don't want the skins to split – try to keep them as dry as possible inside. Once a skewer goes into them easily, drain them.

2. As soon as you can bear to touch them, remove the skins. Purée the flesh, either through a potato ricer or by grating using a fine cheese grater. You want to avoid ending up with any lumps, while still keeping the potato light and fluffy (so no mashing here). Add the egg yolk and salt, and mix gently by hand. Sprinkle 30g/3⅔tbsp of the flour over the potato, and mix together until combined. If the mixture is unmanageably sticky, add the extra flour.

3. Shape the dough into a log, and then slice and roll into marble-sized balls; you should have about 20. Place a ball on your thumb and roll it over the back of a fork. Place on a plate that is sprinkled with a little flour. Repeat with the rest of the dough. You can store these in the fridge for a couple of hours if you need to (covered loosely with some plastic wrap), or you can cook them straight away.

4. Bring a large pot of water to the boil, then add a generous pinch of salt. In a dry saucepan, toast the walnuts until dark brown and fragrant, then chop roughly and set aside. Heat the oil in the pan and fry the sage leaves until crisp, then set aside. Wipe out the pan, and then melt the Gorgonzola into the cream, stirring until it all comes together. Keep over a very low heat until the gnocchi is ready.

5. Reduce the large pot of water to a very gentle simmer, and drop in the gnocchi. Once they begin to float, count to ten, and then scoop them out of the water with a slotted spoon. Drain for a moment, then drop into the cheese sauce, and stir until each gnoccho is coated. Tip into a bowl, and top with the walnuts, sage leaves, and plenty of black pepper. Eat immediately.

Pear and cardamom crisp

FRUIT

10g/2tsp butter
10g/2½tsp light brown sugar
1 large pear
2 pods cardamom, cracked open, seeds crushed to a powder

CRUMBLE

30g/3⅔tbsp plain/all-purpose flour
30g/2tbsp butter
15g/4tsp light brown sugar
15g/2tbsp oats
A couple of walnuts, chopped

EQUIPMENT

10cm/4in-wide ramekin or small ovenproof dish

In her inimitable book on fruit, Jane Grigson writes that 'most people have never eaten a decent pear in their lives'. She's probably right. I love their taste, but I could count on one hand the times that a pear has been perfectly sweet, yielding, and juicy. Happily, they respond very well to a little heat, and a single pear, unripened in the fruit bowl, makes for a glorious dessert.

Serves 1

1. Preheat the oven to 160C fan/350F/gas 4. Melt the butter in a small saucepan, and add the sugar. Peel the pear, slice through the middle, and scoop out the core. Cut into thick slices. Once the butter and sugar are bubbling, add the cardamom pods, then place the pear in the pan, and cook for a couple of minutes.

2. Remove the pear slices and place in a ramekin. Continue to cook the sugar and butter until thick and sticky. Pour it over the pear.

3. Rub together the flour and butter for the crumble with your fingertips until it resembles breadcrumbs. Mix in the sugar, oats, and walnuts.

4. Dampen your hands with cold water, then squeeze bits of crumble together with your fingertips (to encourage it to clump a little). Tip the crumble over the pears. Transfer to the oven for 25 minutes, until golden brown on top. Serve with vanilla ice cream or custard.

Fish suppers in Narnia

There was a jug of creamy milk for the children (Mr. Beaver stuck to beer) and a great big lump of deep yellow butter in the middle of the table from which everyone took as much as he wanted to go with his potatoes and all the children thought—and I agree with them— that there's nothing to beat good freshwater fish if you eat it when it has been alive half an hour ago and has come out of the pan half a minute ago.
The Lion, the Witch and the Wardrobe, C. S. Lewis

On cold, grey winter nights, when rain has been drumming against the windows all day, and the sun never quite shows herself in the sky, I crave fish and chips for tea. I want a parcel of them, soaked in sharp vinegar, with enough salt to make my lips sting. For years I lived around the corner from a marvellous chippie in London, one where the fish was always fresh, the mushy peas were lurid green, and the chips were perfect. I miss it – especially in January. In my kitchen, fish and potatoes are the ultimate deep-winter comfort food. I think this may have something to do with the Pevensies.

When Lucy, Susan, Peter, and Edmund step through the back of the wardrobe into Narnia, they enter a world of perpetual winter, one without even the promise of Christmas to look forward to. They've stolen ill-fitting fur coats (although technically, as the world is in the wardrobe, they're not really stealing at all), and have walked for miles through the snow, traumatized along the way by the horrifying discovery of Mr Tumnus's disappearance. When they sit down to dinner in the Beavers' dam, it's with a tangible sense of relief. This meal of fish and potatoes is the last bit of comfort they see for a while – a meal to be savoured.

Realistically, fish caught, cooked, and consumed within half an hour is not on the cards for most of us. I've managed it only a handful of times: standing ankle-deep in the sea with my cousins as we fought against the waves to reel in flathead before cooking it over a barbeque. In winter, I can't imagine that being quite so pleasant. Happily, fish and potatoes are a dream combination whatever time you have to hand, and however you fancy putting them together.

Herbed fish pie

800g/1¾lb floury
potatoes (Maris Pipers
are perfect)
1tsp salt
80g/⅓ cup butter
100ml/scant ½ cup milk
1tbsp chopped tarragon
1tbsp chopped parsley

PIE FILLING
60g/¼ cup butter
60g/scant ½ cup plain/
all-purpose flour
300ml/1¼ cups milk
250ml/1 cup fish or
vegetable stock
Salt and white pepper
1tsp English mustard
200g/7oz smoked
haddock
200g/7oz salmon
200g/7oz cod
150g/5½oz peeled raw
prawns/shrimp
200g/1⅔ cups frozen
peas

It took a while for me to come around to fish pie – I wrote it off early on after tasting only flavourless and mushy versions. It was game changing to discover that putting the fish and peas into the white sauce raw ensures you don't end up with overcooked fish when you finally take it out of the oven. Play around with whatever combination of fish works for you; I like the contrast in textures and flavours that a mix of smoked fish, oily fish, white fish, and shellfish provides.

Serves 6

1. Preheat the oven to 180C fan/400F/gas 6. Peel the potatoes and chop into evenly sized chunks. Place in a pan and cover with cold water. Bring to the boil, add the salt, then simmer for 10 minutes until soft. Drain, then mash while still hot. Add the butter and milk, and stir to combine. Taste and season with more salt if needed.

2. For the filling, melt the butter in a saucepan, and stir in the flour. Cook, stirring frequently, for a couple of minutes, and then gradually whisk in the milk. Add the stock, and continue stirring over a moderate heat until thick enough to coat the back of a spoon. Take off the heat and season with salt, pepper, and the mustard.

3. Chop the fish into equal chunks. Stir the fish, prawns, and frozen peas through the sauce, then pour it into a pie dish or small roasting tin. Stir the chopped herbs through the cooled mash, and spoon it over the filling. Scrape a fork through the potato to create an uneven surface.

4. Transfer to the oven for 40 minutes, until golden brown on top.

Grilled sea bass with pickled fennel and potato gratin

I could eat potato gratin at any point of the day, with just about anything alongside it. Here, the crispy fish skin and crunchy pickled fennel – a take on Diana Henry's recipe in *Salt Sugar Smoke* – provide the perfect contrast to meltingly soft potatoes. The gratin needs time in the oven, but you can bake it in advance, and then reheat it for twenty minutes when you're ready to serve.

Serves 6

1. To prepare the fennel, blanch the slices in salted boiling water for no more than 30 seconds. Cool immediately under cold water, and pat dry. Bring the vinegar, sugar, fennel seeds, and peppercorns to a simmer in a saucepan, and stir until the sugar has dissolved. Simmer for a further 10 minutes. Put the fennel and dill into a jar or a bowl for serving and cover with the vinegar and spices.

2. For the gratin, preheat the oven to 160C fan/350F/gas 4. Place all the ingredients into a large saucepan. Bring to a very gentle simmer, and cook for 15 minutes – you want the potato to soften a little, but not fall apart. Turn off the heat, and tip the contents into a large roasting dish, rearranging the potato slices to even out the top. Transfer to the oven and bake for an hour and 20 minutes.

3. While the gratin is cooking, take the fish out of any packaging, and place it on a plate in the fridge skin-side up, to dry out a little – this helps the skin to crisp.

4. Take the gratin out of the oven and leave to cool slightly while you cook the fish. Season the skin with salt and pepper. Heat the oil in a frying pan and, when it is smoking, place the fish in, skin-side down. It will want to curl up, so press it down with a fish slice for 30 seconds. Try not to move the fish around too much, but take a peek at the skin after a couple of minutes. Once it is golden brown and crisp, carefully turn it over, and cook for another minute or two. Serve immediately, with the gratin and fennel alongside.

PICKLED FENNEL
1 bulb fennel, finely sliced
300ml/1¼ cups cider vinegar
80g/scant ½ cup granulated sugar
1tbsp fennel seeds
1tbsp peppercorns
A handful of dill fronds

POTATO GRATIN
1.25kg/2¾lb waxy potatoes, sliced into thin discs (I use a mandoline, but slicing finely with a knife would be fine)
250ml/1 cup double/heavy cream
250ml/1 cup milk
2 cloves garlic, finely chopped
A generous grating of nutmeg
1tsp English mustard
Salt and black pepper

FISH
6 skin-on sea bass fillets
1tbsp vegetable oil

Roasted mackerel, potatoes, horseradish, and capers

800g/1¾lb small
potatoes
2 heads broccoli
4tbsp capers
3tbsp olive oil
Salt and black pepper
6 medium or 3 large
mackerel, gutted and
cleaned
2tbsp grated
horseradish
Juice of 1 lemon

SAUCE
150g/⅔ cup crème
fraîche/sour cream
2tbsp grated
horseradish
Juice of 1 lemon

This is a relatively simple supper, especially if you can get
your fishmonger to prepare the fish for you. It's a lovely
dish to put down in the middle of the table, if mid-week
guests (or Pevensies) come to call.

Serves 6

1. Chop any potatoes larger than a walnut into a couple of
pieces, and bring to a simmer in a saucepan of salted water.
Cook for 10 minutes, then drain.

2. Heat the oven to 200C fan/425F/gas 7. Chop the broccoli
into small florets, and arrange around the edges of a
roasting dish. Tip the boiled potatoes and capers into the
centre, then drizzle everything with the olive oil, and
season generously.

3. Make three cuts into the side of each fish, and fill these
with the horseradish. Season the inside of the fish with
pepper and a squeeze of lemon, and the outside with salt.
Lay on top of the potatoes.

4. Place the tray in the oven, and roast for 25 minutes.
Remove the fish from the pan, increase the heat to 220C
fan/475F/gas 9, toss the vegetables together, and return to
the oven for an additional 10 minutes. Pull the fillets away
from the central backbone, and pull any errant bones out
with tweezers or your fingers. Mix the sauce ingredients
together in a bowl.

5. Place the fillets back over the vegetables, and bring the
pan to the table, along with the sauce.

Winter pickles

'Do you think housewives would buy another woman's kimchi?'
'Why not! Don't you think I make good kimchi? My family cook made
the finest pickles in Pyongyang.'
Pachinko, Min Jin Lee

There's little doubt that summer is the more natural time of year to be pickling. There is bountiful produce on offer, but I find that I never want to stand too long over the hob when it's hot. Instead, it's leisurely winter afternoons that I want to spend surrounded by mismatched jars and the scent of vinegar and sugar. To restrict your pickling to summer means missing out on wintery citrus fruit, or fiery kimchi made from crisp cabbages.

I keep endless jars of pickles and preserves in my cupboard, and regularly find myself reaching for them when pulling together a quick lunch. Though they take time to prepare, they're worth the investment: a batch can last you for months and will provide a happy companion to innumerable dishes. They're an ideal use for a glut of vegetables too – if you're forever finding half-eaten, rotten cucumbers or mouldy carrots at the bottom of your fridge drawer, consider extending their life by pickling while they're still fresh. Once sealed up in jars, the key to pickles is time. Though I technically shouldn't advise you to do so, I've left unopened jars for years, happening across them during a kitchen clear-out, and digging into them long after anything else would be inedible.

It is time, too, that pickles require on the page. The women in *Pachinko*, who make as many jars of kimchi as their small kitchen can handle, spend their days preparing the pickle, then waiting for it to age. *Little Women*'s Amy's pickled limes, revered at school and passed secretly under desks during morning lessons, were likely made many months before, then preserved in brine and sent in ships across the Atlantic. Mrs Glover's famous piccalilli, kept for the winter, and requested by the doctor who delivers Ursula in *Life After Life* (again and again), prompts him to refer to her as 'she of the excellent pickles'. These are wonderful books to read while your vinegar simmers away; with the chill of winter in their pages and a focus on the passage of time.

Pickled limes

I have been intrigued by these limes ever since I first read Amy March declare that the girls at school had decided it was 'nothing but limes now'. My experience with pickled limes was based solely on the ones I'd seen served alongside curries in our local Indian. Unsurprisingly, Amy's limes were nothing like this. Fresh fruit was heavily taxed during the American Civil War, but whole pickled limes were widely available. The sugar takes some of the sour edge off the fruit, making them taste something like the sour, tangy sweets enjoyed in classrooms today.

Makes 8 limes

1. Wash the limes well – only use unblemished ones without broken skins. Pack them into a 1-litre/34oz jar.

2. Put the salt, sugar, and water into a saucepan, and stir over a low heat until the salt and sugar have dissolved. Allow to cool, then pour over the limes.

3. Store in the fridge for at least a month, before eating the limes one by one, or sharing them with only your most deserving friends.

8 unwaxed limes
40g/3tbsp rock salt
80g/scant ½ cup granulated sugar
400ml/1¾ cups water

Kimchi

1 Chinese cabbage
100g/½ cup rock salt
150g/5½oz radishes
6 spring onions/
scallions
A bunch of chives
4tbsp gochujang paste
2tsp grated ginger
2tsp grated garlic

I vividly remember the first time I ate Korean food. It was 2012, and I was with my mum in New York. We had walked for miles, and found ourselves in a strip of restaurants ordering bowls of fried rice with fiery kimchi tossed through it. I've loved it ever since. When reading Min Jin Lee's *Pachinko*, I found myself craving its unique salty, spicy flavour, dreaming of it folded into a barely set omelette, or stirred through noodles covered in broth.

Makes a 1-litre/34oz jar

1. Rinse the cabbage leaves and cut into long strips. Pat them dry with kitchen towel, then place in a colander. Sprinkle over the salt and toss a little so it's evenly distributed, then place a plate on top of the cabbage, and weight it down with a couple of tins. Leave for 3 hours.

2. Rinse and squeeze the cabbage, and place it in a large mixing bowl. Cut the radishes into fine batons, the spring onions into thin strips, and roughly chop the chives. Toss together.

3. In a small bowl, mix together the gochujang paste, ginger, and garlic. Stir this through the cabbage mix, until all the vegetables are coated. Squash into a 2-litre/68oz jar or container with a good seal, and leave at room temperature for 3 days, checking it daily and squashing down the cabbage so that it all sits under the liquid that has leached out of the leaves.

4. After 3 days, transfer it to a smaller 1-litre/34oz jar or container and store in the fridge. It will be ready to eat after another 3 days, and is best consumed within a month once it's been opened.

Piccalilli

200g/7oz shallots
100g/3½oz green beans
½ medium cauliflower
150g/5½oz cucumber, deseeded
150g/5½oz carrots
100g/½ cup rock salt
500ml/2 cups cider vinegar
1tbsp ground turmeric
2tsp ground ginger
1tbsp ground coriander/cilantro
1tbsp ground cumin
1tsp hot English mustard powder
2 cloves garlic, finely chopped
2tbsp mustard seeds
150g/¾ cup granulated sugar
20g/3tbsp cornflour/cornstarch

I don't want to play pickle favourites but, if I did, it would be this. I love its lurid yellow colour, the crunch of the vegetables and the way it works so gloriously with cheese on toast. It's eaten over and over again in *Life After Life* – with ham, as snow falls thickly outside. It's exactly the sort of circumstance under which it should be eaten, spooned mouthful by mouthful onto buttered toast topped with thick slices of leftover Christmas ham.

Makes enough to fill 3 x 400g/14oz jars

1. First, chop the vegetables. They should all be roughly the same size, so cut the peeled shallots into 4 pieces, chop the beans, chop the cauliflower florets off the stalks, slice the cucumber and carrot into even lengths, and then dice.

2. Put the vegetables into a mixing bowl. Sprinkle over the salt, and toss through. Cover with a tea towel and leave in a cool place overnight. The salt will draw some of the moisture out, and begin the pickling.

3. Transfer the vegetables to a sieve and rinse under cold running water for 3 minutes to get rid of the salt. Pour the vinegar and spices into a saucepan, and bring to a simmer. Tip in the rinsed vegetables, and cook at a slow boil for 10 minutes. Piccalilli is not chutney; it should still have a bite to it, so don't cook the vegetables for too long.

4. Scoop the vegetables out of the vinegar, and place back in the mixing bowl. Off the heat, pour the sugar into the hot vinegar and stir until dissolved. Turn the heat back on.

5. Dilute the cornflour in a small bowl with a couple of tablespoons of the vinegar. Whisk until you have a smooth paste. Pour the paste into the simmering vinegar, and whisk through. The mixture will thicken. Pour this over the vegetables, and stir.

6. Spoon the piccalilli into sterilized jars (see p. 158). Ideally, you should leave the jars for 1–3 months for the flavours to develop, but I'm notoriously unable to wait that long.

Afternoons with the oven on

There is a piece of cake on a plate in front of her. It is dense, moist, almost black; it is spiked with liqueur, and wet with apricot preserve. There is the scent of almonds, a silver fork on a brocade napkin, a strawberry cut and splayed into almost a flower.
Melmoth, Sarah Perry

When I first moved to the UK, our energy provider made an error with the gas bills. It was eventually rectified, but for nearly five years I was under the impression that gas was exponentially more expensive than electricity, and quite literally out of my price range. And so, on cold days in my flat, I'd turn on our electric oven and stand uncomfortably close to it in order to keep warm. Somehow, I managed to justify the cost of ingredients (but not the cost of central heating) and would spend long afternoons baking, the backs of my legs pressed against the oven door. After I'd creamed butter and sugar, and the batter had been placed in the oven, I'd sit on the floor to be near the warmth, and lose myself in a novel until the harsh beep of my phone alerted me to the now-risen cake.

The books I read on these afternoons were almost invariably slim tomes, ones that flew along at a cracking pace, and could be devoured in a single day, or by the time the icing was dry on the cake. Murder mysteries, Conan Doyle short stories, gripping Gothic horror – I'm not very good at handling scarier stories, but the comforting smell of a cake behind me was always a help.

I still love baking cakes. Even though I don't have much of a sweet tooth, I've long been aware that cakes fill the kitchen with both literal and figurative warmth. They're almost always too large for a family, or a couple of flatmates, and so beg to be shared. Whether showy, or homely, they suggest that you've made an effort. In the colder months, I fancy a specific sort of cake. Light sponges make sense in spring and summer, but when it's grey and bleak outside I want heavy cakes, dense with nuts, or with rich chocolate icing. The kind of cakes that warm you in more ways than one.

Rose and pistachio cake

On visiting Istanbul one rainy weekend, I set out to find the start of the Orient Express train line. I was on the hunt for the exact spot where Hercule Poirot stood, trying to charm his way onto an already packed train. When I found it, I could see him standing there, a set of matching luggage piled neatly next to him, hat perched jauntily on his head.* A journey on the famous train itself is little more than a pipe dream, but I did manage to wander the markets in Istanbul, collecting ingredients for a cake I can imagine my favourite Orient Express passenger nibbling away at.

Serves 10

1. Preheat the oven to 160C fan/350F/gas 4 and grease and line the base of the cake tin with parchment paper.

2. Cream the butter and sugar together until light and creamy. Beat in the eggs, one at a time. Blitz the pistachio nuts in a food processor until finely ground, then fold into the batter along with the almonds.

3. Add the orange zest to the batter, then the orange juice along with the rosewater. Finally, fold in the flour.

4. Spoon the mixture into the tin, and place in the oven for 50 minutes. Cover the top of the tin with foil for the last 10 minutes if it's browning too quickly. Check the cake is cooked by placing a skewer into the centre – it should come out clean.

5. While the cake is cooling, beat the butter and icing sugar together until thick and creamy. Add the lemon juice. Spread the icing over the top of the cooled cake, and scrape it down the sides a little. Decorate with the rose petals and chopped pistachio nuts.

* I realized, years later, I was standing in the wrong station. Of course.

CAKE
250g/1 cup butter
250g/1¼ cups caster/superfine sugar
3 eggs
100g/¾ cup shelled and peeled pistachio nuts
100g/1 cup ground almonds
Zest and juice of 1 orange
1tsp rosewater
60g/scant ½ cup plain/all-purpose flour

ICING
80g/⅓ cup butter
250g/1¾ cups icing/confectioner's sugar
1tbsp lemon juice
Rose petals and chopped pistachio nuts, to decorate

EQUIPMENT
20cm/8in loose-bottomed cake tin/pan
Food processor

Blood orange cake

CRYSTALLIZED BLOOD
ORANGES
150g/¾ cup caster/
superfine sugar
100ml/scant ½ cup
water
2 blood oranges, sliced
into thin rounds

CAKE
200g/¾ cup + 2tbsp
butter
150g/¾ cup caster/
superfine sugar
3 eggs
110g/¾ cup + 1½tbsp
plain/all-purpose flour
4tbsp sour cream
200g/2 cups ground
almonds
2tsp baking powder

TO SERVE
Sour cream or yoghurt

EQUIPMENT
20cm/8in loose-
bottomed cake tin/pan

I have been reading Conan Doyle's Sherlock Holmes stories for decades; they're so comfortingly familiar now. They're also the source of my most intangible literary inspiration: the five orange pips that indicate imminent death sent me straight to the kitchen in search of something I could do with blood oranges. It's a silly link, I know, but I make no apologies for the cake, which I borrowed from my friend Aoife. It's lovely with any sort of orange, but it's the perfect vehicle for the season's star fruit: blood oranges.

Serves 10

1. Line your cake tin; you'll need to do it with butter and parchment paper to ensure you don't lose any of the lovely orange syrup. Heat your oven to 160C fan/350F/gas 4.

2. Prepare the crystallized blood oranges. Put the sugar and water in a shallow pan, and stir over a medium heat until the sugar melts. Turn up the heat, add the orange slices and cook until very soft. Place the slices on some parchment paper to cool, and reduce the syrup (which should now be a glorious orange-pink) to the thickness of golden syrup.

3. To make the cake, beat the butter and sugar until light and creamy. Add the eggs one at a time, with a spoonful of the flour to stop the mixture curdling, and beat. Mix in the sour cream.

4. Fold the almonds into the mixture, then sieve in the rest of the flour and baking powder. Fold in very gently, and stop as soon as the mixture is combined.

5. Paint the syrup over the base of your lined tin, and tessellate the orange slices on top. Spoon the cake batter over the oranges and smooth out the top. Transfer the tin to the oven for an hour, or until a skewer inserted in the cake comes out clean.

6. Cool the cake in the tin and then invert it onto a serving plate. Remove the paper (making sure not to take any of the orange slices with it). Serve with sour cream or yoghurt.

Sachertorte

CAKE
200g/7oz dark/
bittersweet chocolate
150g/⅔ cup butter
150g/¾ cup caster/
superfine sugar
5 eggs, separated
75g/¾ cup ground
almonds
100g/¾ cup plain/
all-purpose flour

JAM
150g/½ cup apricot
jam/jelly
2tbsp orange liqueur

ICING
100g/3½oz dark/
bittersweet chocolate
150g/¾ cup caster/
superfine sugar
80ml/⅓ cup water

EQUIPMENT
20cm/8in loose-
bottomed or spring-
form cake tin/pan

This cake – the kind that people sit back from with an exhausted look on their face – only makes sense in winter. In Sarah Perry's gloriously dark *Melmoth* there is a slice of cake described in such glorious detail that it doesn't need to be named. This is probably hopelessly inauthentic, but it's still completely delicious.

Serves 12

1. Preheat the oven to 160C fan/350F/gas 4 and grease and line a cake tin. Melt the chocolate in a heatproof bowl over a pan of simmering water.

2. Beat the butter and 100g/ ½ cup of the sugar until light and creamy. Beat in the egg yolks, one at a time, and then the cooled chocolate. Fold in the almonds and flour.

3. In a spotlessly clean bowl, beat the egg whites until they form very soft peaks. Slowly pour in the remaining 50g/ ¼ cup of sugar, and beat until stiff peaks form.

4. Stir a third of the egg whites into the batter to loosen, and then gently fold in the rest. Pour into the tin and bake for 55 minutes to an hour, until the cake is well risen, and a skewer inserted into the centre comes out clean.

5. Cool in the tin for an hour, then remove from the tin and invert it on a cooling rack. Leave to cool completely.

6. Place the rack over a baking sheet. Melt the jam in a saucepan (passing it through a sieve if it has chunks), and add the liqueur. Paint all over the cake using a pastry brush.

7. To make the icing, combine the ingredients in a pan, and bring to a gentle simmer over a low heat. Simmer until it reaches 112C/234F, or soft ball stage, then leave to sit for a minute. Slowly pour the icing over the cake, making sure it drips down the edges. Allow to set, then serve with heaps of softly whipped cream.

Whisky and water

Sherlock Holmes requests his whisky with water in *A Study in Scarlet*. Unsurprisingly, he's 'right': it's been scientifically proven to be the best way to drink whisky.* My recreation of the smoky Baker Street flat replaces the water with a dash of smoky tea, making this the perfect cocktail for a brisk winter afternoon spent by the oven.

Serves 2

1. Pour the water over the tea and leave to brew for 4 minutes. Add the sugar, stirring to dissolve it in the hot tea. Strain the tea into a mug, and chill in the fridge.

2. Divide the whisky between 2 glasses. Peel 2 strips of zest from the lemon, then juice it and add 2 teaspoons of juice to the tea.

3. Stir, then divide the tea between the whisky glasses. Add the zest, and serve.

* I'm entirely serious here: extensive research was undertaken by Björn C. G. Karlsson and Ran Friedman, who concluded that the flavour of whisky is improved when the alcohol molecules are mixed with water molecules.

60ml/¼ cup freshly boiled water
2tsp Lapsang Souchong tea (or 2 tea bags)
2tsp caster/superfine sugar
120ml/½ cup Scotch whisky
1 lemon

Meals with someone special

Many people looked at Carol, however, because she was generally the most attractive woman in the room. And Therese was so delighted to be with her, so proud of her, she looked at no one else but Carol. Then as she read the menu, Carol would slowly press Therese's foot under the table to make her smile.
The Price of Salt, Patricia Highsmith

During my teenage years, in the absence of a love story of my own, I lost myself in fictional ones. I sat in drawing rooms with Elinor Dashwood and Edward Ferras. I fell in love with George Emerson over a dinner table in Florence. My heart broke for the English patient, and his memories of Katharine Clifton. I took a seat in a Manhattan restaurant alongside Carol Aird and Therese Belivet. I agonized with Stevens as he recalled lost moments with Miss Kenton. I swooned at the letter sent from Frederick Wentworth to Anne Elliot.

Now in my thirties, I am yet to fall in love. I've had unrequited crushes, gone out with people I've fancied, and been on some wonderfully terrible dates, all as I've watched friends around me move in with their partners, celebrate weddings, and have children. When it's cold, and dark, and people are curled up at home on the sofa with their partners, being single can feel lonely. Sometimes I relish evenings in alone, but, every now and then, what I want most is to cook something fancy to share with someone I love. My favourite literary romances see plenty of large group dinners, but to spend a meal with just one person – as Jane Eyre does with Rochester by the fire, or Therese and Carol enjoy doing at restaurants – is a statement.

Though I remain single, I have built the long-term, meaningful relationships I longed for in my teens in other ways. I have fallen in platonic love multiple times – sometimes gradually, and occasionally all at once, in a heady rush. I have met people I know I'll still be talking to when I'm ninety. I may not have one defining relationship, but instead have many. I relish these relationships, and though my life doesn't look the way I imagined it would, it is certainly full of people with whom I can share a special meal.

Duck leg, pancetta, pomegranate and puy lentils

2 duck legs (thigh and drumstick)

1tbsp groundnut oil

75g/½ cup diced pancetta

2 banana shallots, sliced

2 cloves garlic, minced

80g/½ cup puy lentils

100ml/scant ½ cup vermouth

200ml/generous ¾ cup chicken stock

2tbsp pomegranate molasses

Salt and black pepper

Seeds from half a pomegranate

This is a wonderfully easy one-pot dinner – simple to put together, leaving you to sip cocktails in another room as it finishes cooking in the oven. Both rich and warming, it's a lovely, cosy, wintery supper for two. A herb salad alongside would be perfect.

Serves 2

1. Preheat the oven to 180C fan/400 F/gas 6. Take the duck from the fridge, unwrap it, and dry the skin with kitchen paper. Warm the groundnut oil in a pan (one with a lid that can be transferred to the oven is ideal), and place the duck legs into it, skin-side down. Fry until the skin is crispy and golden, and then flip over and cook for a further 10 minutes on the other side. Remove the duck to a plate.

2. Add the pancetta to the pan, and fry for 5 minutes until golden. Remove from the pan and set aside, leaving the fat behind.

3. Fry the shallots over a medium heat for 5 minutes until softened. Add the garlic and fry for a further couple of minutes, until the garlic smells fragrant.

4. Tip the lentils into the pan, and stir through the shallots. Pour in the vermouth and allow it to bubble away for a minute or two before adding the stock and pomegranate molasses and some seasoning. Nestle the duck legs, skin-side up, into the lentils, and place a lid on the pan. Alternatively, if your pan won't go into the oven, transfer everything to an ovenproof dish, and cover.

5. Bake in the oven for an hour, then remove the lid and cook for a final 10 minutes. Keep an eye on it to ensure the lentils don't dry out.

6. Serve sprinkled with pomegranate seeds, alongside a herb salad – large parsley and rocket leaves dressed with olive oil and cider vinegar would be ideal.

Cheese soufflé

When you're hoping to impress, there are few more successful ways of doing so than baking a cheese soufflé. Notoriously unpredictable and temperamental (though actually eminently manageable, if you approach it with a light hand and a preheated oven), it's a dish that tastes fantastic, looks beautiful, and is such fun to eat.

Serves 2

1. Preheat the oven to 200C fan/425F/gas 7. Prepare your dishes. Grease 2 ramekins generously, then sprinkle in the Parmesan and breadcrumbs. Turn the ramekins so that the cheese and bread stick to the butter, coating the sides and base.

2. Melt the butter in a small pan, and add the flour. Whisk over a low heat for 3 minutes. Add the milk a splash at a time, whisking constantly to keep it smooth. Take the sauce off the heat, and season with the mustard, cayenne pepper, and thyme.

3. Whisk the egg yolk in a small bowl, and then pour in the white sauce, whisking constantly. Stir the cheese through.

4. Whisk the egg whites to stiff peaks in a spotlessly clean bowl. Mix a third of the whites into the cheese sauce to loosen it, and then gently fold in the rest. Divide the batter between the ramekins.

5. Put the ramekins in a roasting dish, and transfer the dish to the oven. Before you close the door, pour boiling water into the tray until it comes halfway up the sides of the ramekins. Bake for 12 minutes until risen, and browned on top.

6. While the soufflés are baking, prepare the salad. Whisk the vinegar and mustard with the seasoning, and then slowly add the olive oil, whisking constantly. Toss the leaves in the dressing, and serve alongside the soufflés.

PREPARING THE DISHES
1tbsp butter
1tsp grated Parmesan
1tsp breadcrumbs

SOUFFLÉ
1tbsp butter
1tbsp plain/all-purpose flour
60ml/¼ cup milk
½tsp English mustard
¼tsp cayenne pepper
Leaves from 3 sprigs thyme
1 egg yolk
60g/⅔ cup grated mature/sharp Cheddar
30g/½ cup grated Parmesan (or a vegetarian alternative)
2 egg whites

AND
½tsp white wine vinegar
½tsp English mustard
Salt and black pepper
1tsp olive oil
Mix of leaves and herbs (watercress, pea shoots, rocket/arugula, lamb's lettuce)

EQUIPMENT
2 x 10cm/4in ramekins

Star anise and pink peppercorn crème brûlée

This is classy, pretty, and entirely delicious. It's also extraordinarily satisfying – cracking a spoon through the crisp crust of caramel into the velvety custard below is a uniquely wonderful feeling. Best of all, you can make the majority of the dessert the night before, and then add the caramel topping just before you serve it.

Serves 2

1. Preheat the oven to 140C fan/325F/gas 2. Put the milk, cream, peppercorns and star anise in a small saucepan. Place over a low heat until it starts to simmer around the edges, but make sure it doesn't boil. Take off the heat and leave for 20 minutes to infuse.

2. Whisk the egg yolks and sugar together in a bowl until light and creamy. Strain the milk and cream into the egg yolks (so you leave the peppercorns and star anise behind), whisking constantly as you do.

3. Divide the custard between 2 ramekins, place in a roasting dish, and put in the middle of the oven. Before you close the door, fill the roasting dish with hot water to create a bain-marie – this will allow the crème brûlée to cook more evenly, resulting in a smoother, silkier texture. Bake for 45 minutes, but keep an eye on it after 35 minutes – you're cooking it at a very low temperature, so if your oven runs a little warm it will make a big difference. When cooked, the centre of the custard should be only very slightly wobbly.

4. Once you have taken the dish from the oven, remove the ramekins, and leave to cool. Once cool to the touch, cover with plastic wrap and chill completely in the fridge.

5. Remove from the fridge 30 minutes before you'd like to serve them. Just before serving, sprinkle a thin, even layer of sugar over the top. With a blowtorch, or under a searingly hot grill, melt the sugar until a dark, rich amber.

60ml/¼ cup milk
200ml/generous ¾ cup double/heavy cream
20 pink peppercorns
3 star anise
3 egg yolks
2tbsp golden caster/ superfine sugar (plus 1tbsp extra for the top)

EQUIPMENT
2 x 10cm/4in ramekins

Baskets full of dumplings

'Time to eat,' Auntie An-mei happily announces, bringing out a steaming pot of the wonton she was just wrapping. There are piles of food on the table, served buffet style, just like at the Kweilin feasts.
The Joy Luck Club, Amy Tan

On Sunday mornings in Brisbane, my sister and I would beg to be taken out for dim sum. I remember so clearly the large dining room, the smell of the jasmine tea, the heavily starched white tablecloths covered in paper, the steamed pork dumplings that we ordered each time without fail, and the lazy Susan in the centre of the table that we'd spin as fast as we dared while mum wasn't looking. If we were lucky, our cousins or granny would join us too. The more people around the table, the more dishes we'd be able to taste.

The best time to visit was around Chinese New Year; which (now that I'm on the other side of the world) falls late in winter, just before spring starts to return. Three floors below the restaurant, in Chinatown, strings of firecrackers were on sale, a giant puppet dragon danced through the street, and we'd stop and get tiny panda biscuits or fish-shaped pastries from the packed shelves of the Chinese supermarket. On the night itself, our local Chinese restaurant, though smaller than the huge one in town, would set off firecrackers on the street – the sound and the smoke would bring us onto the deck of my dad's house, from where we could watch the sky light up.

To this day, a generous spread of Chinese food on the table remains an incredibly welcome sight. For the most part it's not fast food, but the kind that asks for a bit of your time. It's also food that benefits from a community behind it – a production line of people wrapping, folding and sealing the dumplings closed. I tend to make it when I have a big crew of people around. It's food that makes me miss my family, and the camaraderie and companionship of cooking around Mum's granite kitchen island. It's why I adore Amy Tan's collection of Chinese-American women in *The Joy Luck Club*; whatever their history, they continue to gather together to play mah jong, and to cook and eat dishes that are best shared.

Garlic and sesame greens

I did say that the food in this section takes time, but this dish is the work of moments. It's a great accompaniment to a piece of grilled fish, a steak, or a curry, but I most often eat big bowls of it on its own, or with a little bowl of steamed rice alongside. When I've been out of the house for a while, especially if I haven't found access to a kitchen somewhere and had the chance to cook my own food, it's the dish I come home craving.

Serves 4 as a side, or 2 as a meal

1. Prep all the veg – top and tail the beans, take the ends off the pak choi and cut it into strips; rinse anything that needs a little attention.

2. Whisk the sauce ingredients together, and have them ready beside the hob before you start cooking.

3. Place a wok, or wide pan, over a high heat. Drop the sesame seeds in, and move them around for 30 seconds, until they turn a golden brown. Remove and keep to one side.

4. Warm the sesame oil until it starts to smoke, and then drop in the hard stalks of the pak choi. Stir fry for a minute or two, moving them around the pan, and then add the beans. After another couple of minutes, add the mangetout and the pak choi leaves.

5. Once everything is a bright, vibrant green, pour in the sauce. Cook for a final minute, stirring constantly.

6. Serve immediately, topped with the toasted sesame seeds.

GREENS

100g/3½oz green beans
2 pak choi/bok choy
100g/1 cup mangetout/snow peas
1tbsp sesame oil

SAUCE

2 cloves garlic, crushed
1tbsp dark soya sauce
1tbsp oyster sauce (or a vegetarian oyster sauce)
1tsp chilli sauce (sweet or spicy, depending on your taste)
1tsp sesame oil

AND

1tbsp sesame seeds

Wonton soup

WONTONS

15g/½ cup dried shiitake mushrooms

2tsp sesame oil

A thumb-sized piece of ginger, grated

3 cloves garlic, minced

250g/3½ cups fresh shiitake mushrooms, finely diced

20g/1 cup coriander/cilantro

4 spring onions/scallions, finely sliced

250g/9oz firm tofu, finely diced

1tsp freshly ground white pepper

A large pinch of salt

30–36 wonton wrappers

BROTH

1 litre/4¼ cups chicken or vegetable stock

3 cloves garlic, peeled and roughly chopped

A thumb-sized piece of ginger, roughly sliced

3 banana shallots, roughly sliced

2tbsp Shaoxing rice wine

1tbsp light brown sugar

AND

3 small pak choi/bok choy

2 spring onions/scallions

2tbsp toasted sesame seeds

2tsp sesame oil

The long winter nights

This is my interpretation of *The Joy Luck Club*'s Auntie An-mei's wonton soup. Traditionally, these dumplings would be filled with minced pork and prawn, and though I love the classic, I've become very fond of this tofu and mushroom version. You could, of course, use ready-made frozen wontons, but these are not that tricky to master and, as long as they stay closed when dropped into the water, it doesn't matter one bit if they look a little 'homemade'.

Serves 6, generously

1. First, make the wontons. You can do these a day in advance and store them in the fridge until needed. Rehydrate the dried mushrooms by covering them with boiling water. Leave to steep while you prepare the filling. Warm the sesame oil in a pan, and then add the ginger and garlic. Fry for a couple of minutes, stirring so that it does not brown.

2. Add the fresh mushrooms and fry for 10 minutes over a low heat, until the water they release has cooked off and the mushrooms have browned a little. Add the drained rehydrated mushrooms. Finely chop the stalks from the bunch of coriander (keep the leaves for later) and add to the pan along with the spring onions. Cook for a few minutes.

3. Add the diced tofu, and heat through for a minute. Season, then take off the heat and leave to cool completely in the fridge.

4. Put a teaspoon of the filling onto the centre of each wonton wrapper, wet the edges of the wrapper, and fold it diagonally over the filling to form a triangle. Make sure there's no air trapped inside, then dampen the two side corners, and gently pull them together at the base of the wonton and press firmly to join them. Set the dumplings aside under a damp tea towel.

5. To make the broth, bring the stock to a gentle simmer

with the garlic, ginger, and shallots (don't worry about
chopping them neatly, you'll be straining them out later.
Season with the rice wine and the sugar. Simmer for
10 minutes.

6. Slice the bottoms off the pak choi, and separate the
leaves. Wash, then add to the broth. Cook for 5 minutes,
and then remove with tongs, and divide between the
serving bowls.

7. Bring a pot of water to a very gentle simmer. Drop in the
wontons in batches, ensuring they're not too crowded, and
cook for a couple of minutes. Use a slotted spoon to pull
the wontons out of the water once they float to the top,
and add to the pak choi in the bowls. Strain the broth over
the wontons, and then top with sliced spring onions, the
reserved fresh coriander leaves, a sprinkle of sesame seeds,
and a dribble of sesame oil. Serve immediately.

Char siu bao

I set about making a batch of these one weekend, fully expecting them to prove too tricky to include in this book. But, although they take time, they are entirely delicious, eminently achievable, and the joy of pulling the lid off your own perfectly steamed, gorgeously risen buns is hard to overstate. You can also eat the char siu pork straight out of the oven with rice and stir-fried greens, as Auntie An-mei serves it.

Makes 12

1. About 24 hours before you'd like to make the buns, marinate the pork. Slice the rind off the belly, keeping as much of the fat as you can, then score the meat through the fat, and place into a roasting tray that it fits into snugly. Mix together all other filling ingredients apart from the flour. Pour this over the meat, cover with foil, and place in the fridge overnight (or for at least a couple of hours).

2. The next day, preheat the oven to 140C fan/325F/gas 3. Place the covered pork in the oven, and roast for 4 hours. Check it every hour or so, basting the meat if it's looking dry. After 4 hours, remove the foil, baste once more, and increase the heat to 170C fan/375F/gas 5. Add a splash of water to the pan. Cook for 45 minutes until caramelized.

3. Take the pork out of the oven, and rest for 10 minutes. Pull the meat apart with a couple of forks, drain the sauce from it, and transfer the meat to a bowl. Pour the leftover sauce into a small saucepan, whisk in the flour, and reduce it over a slow heat until thick. Stir the thickened sauce back through the pork and then place in the fridge until cool.

4. To make the dough, put the flour, sugar, and salt into a bowl. Mix the milk, oil, and yeast together, and pour into the flour. Mix by hand and then knead for 10 minutes until soft and elastic. Grease the bowl with a little oil, return the dough to it, cover and set aside to rise for an hour until it's doubled in size, and bounces back when prodded.

FILLING
600g/1lb 5oz pork belly
2 cloves garlic, crushed
2tbsp dark brown sugar
2tbsp dark soy sauce
2tbsp hoisin sauce
1tbsp ketchup
1tbsp rice wine vinegar
1tbsp vegetable oil
1tbsp plain/all-purpose flour

DOUGH
300g/2¼ cups plain/all-purpose flour
40g/scant ¼ cup caster/superfine sugar
A pinch of salt
160ml/⅔ cup milk
2tbsp vegetable oil
18g/1tbsp fresh yeast (or 5g/1tsp easy-action yeast)

TO SERVE
Pickled vegetables (cucumbers in soya and vinegar are lovely, as are pickled Chinese cabbage or carrots)
Soy sauce

5. Divide the dough into 12 equal portions. Roll each into a ball, and then roll out to a disc, around 5mm/¼in thick. Leave the centre thick, and then roll out the edges of the disc a little further, until they're about 2mm/¹⁄₁₆in thick. Place a spoonful of the pork in the centre, and then pleat around the edges to draw them over the pork. The pleats will leave a hole in the centre over the pork, so twist them closed to seal the filling inside. Place on a square of parchment paper, and then leave to rise for 20 minutes.

6. Bring a pan of water to a gentle simmer. Put the bao in a bamboo steamer, leaving some space inbetween as they will expand. Place over the water, and steam for 15 minutes, until risen. These are delicious eaten in batches as the next ones steam, but if you want to serve them later, just warm them through gently in the steamer for a couple of minutes before bringing them to the table. Serve with some sharp pickles and plenty of soy sauce.

More books to keep you company through the chilly winter nights...

Feel a prickle down the back of your neck as you walk the halls of the Overlook Hotel with Danny Torrance in *The Shining*. Accompany Melanie as she moves with her little brother and sister into her tyrannical uncle's home: *The Magic Toyshop*. While away a cold and blustery night onboard the *Pequod* in the company of Ahab, as he hunts down *Moby-Dick*. Join emergency-response ambulance drivers Kay and Mickey on *The Night Watch* in wartime London. In a bid to save them from burning, slip slim tomes into your coat pocket, alongside *The Book Thief*'s Liesel. Follow Jean-Baptiste Grenouille, and his exceptional nose, throughout Paris as he becomes obsessed with *Perfume*, and with murder. Keep a close eye on *The Picture of Dorian Gray* in the attic. Explore the icy streets of East London with Sally Lockhart, Jim Taylor, and Frederick Garland in *The Ruby in the Smoke*. Jump from canal boat to canal boat, and stroll along the towpath, with Margaret: *Thursday's Child*. Experience an overwhelming moral dilemma in the company of Rodion Raskolnikov as he considers *Crime and Punishment*. Dream of Manderley (again) in the company of the second Mrs de Winter, the ice-cold – even in midsummer – Mrs Danvers, and *Rebecca*.

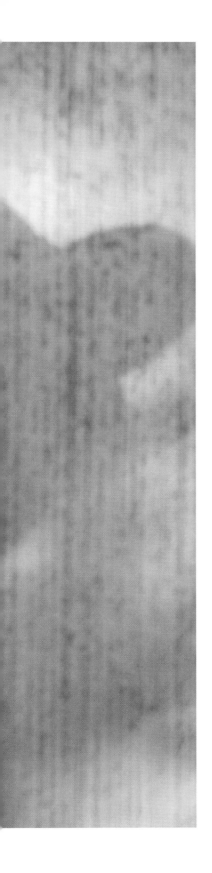

The first
signs of spring

The first signs of spring

'Is the spring coming?' he said. 'What is it like?'...
'It is the sun shining on the rain and the rain falling on the
sunshine...'
The Secret Garden, Frances Hodgson Burnett

The first day of spring always manages to creep up on me. I forget, from year to year, the magic moment when the daffodils start to push their sunny yellow heads through the frigid ground, when the biting chill has gone from the air, and when you can feel the sun hitting your cheekbones, even if your coat is still wrapped warm around you. The richness of spring comes later, but these months are generous in their own way – vibrant winter greens still easily accessible, evenings still cool enough for warming comfort food, bright weekend mornings perfect for leisurely breakfasts in bed. The season is a promise: blossoms opening on trees, grass growing slowly greener and richer as the frost leaves the ground.

I used to spend much of the year longing for autumn, the cool, crisp evenings, abundant apples, the changing leaves, the re-emergence of hats and scarves and gloves. I never gave spring a look-in; before I knew it was here, it would have galloped away from me and summer would have arrived. But then, after one bitterly cold and dreary winter in London, which had left me feeling particularly down, I found myself noticing spring, and welcoming it in with open arms. That year, when England started to come back to life, and threw off her huge winter coat, I re-read *The Secret Garden*. I adore winter, but I had reached the end of it feeling like Mary Lennox and Colin Craven: grey and frail and without any real memory of the warmth of the sun. I remember pushing open the windows and airing out my little flat, willing the still-cool air inside to clear out the memory of the low months. I sought out gorgeously fragrant herbs, and got soil under my fingernails as I repotted them in big boxes for the windowsill. I bought honey, heavy with the scent of local blooms. I lingered over weekend breakfasts, with the crossword and a pot of tea, and cooked with the first of the spring produce.

Emily Dickinson writes of the light that exists in spring, a different light from that which exists at any other point of the year. It's the light at the end of the darkness of winter, that rests differently on the ground, that creeps into corners and illuminates parts of the world that have lain in shadow for months. A light that encourages us to step outside our cosy homes, and back out into the world.

A Light exists in Spring
Not present on the Year
At any other period –
When March is scarcely here

From 'A Light Exists in Spring', Emily Dickinson

Comfort food

...When my brain begins to reel from my literary labors, I make an occasional cheese dip.
A Confederacy of Dunces, John Kennedy Toole

My childhood was a comfortable one: a fiercely close sister, a warm extended family, and plenty of books and time spent in the kitchen. I grew up with a palpable love of home, and so sometimes find it difficult to explain my decision to board a plane to London as soon as I was old enough. Far from running away, I left because my parents had instilled in me a desire to explore the world that lay beyond our suburb. But my first year was tricky; Whitechapel was grey, the mould in our bathroom was pervasive, my commute was endless. I missed home desperately.

I had managed to find myself in a liminal state between one home and the next. And so, while I worked and waited, I became adept at seeking out comfort. I found it in a blanket I bought on a holiday in Mexico, which has followed me from sofa to sofa. I found it in the familiar, reassuring books I grew up with: *I Capture the Castle*, the Harry Potter series, Jane Austen's novels, *The Secret Garden*. I brought comfort into my kitchen with tinned tomato soup, cheese on toast, deep bowls of chicken noodle broth, and buttered soldiers spread with Vegemite and dipped into runny-yolked eggs: food I could make on autopilot, without having to think. And slowly, as I started to think of England as my home, I found I needed to draw on these things less and less.

When I miss my family now, or when anxiety is eating away at me, or when 'my brain begins to reel' (thank you, Ignatius J. Reilly), I still seek out comfort. But my definition of it has broadened; I no longer seek only the comfort of my parents' home, or of childhood, but of memories and of homes I have built here. I remember the cosy nights spent in my friend Jen's old flat, when we cooked jambalaya in a weighty pot on the stove. I remember being inspired by E. L. Konigsburg's *From the Mixed-Up Files of Mrs. Basil E. Frankweiler* to make a deep dish of macaroni cheese one rainy night for the children I used to nanny. And I can measure my life in the various batches of brownies I have baked in whatever pan I had to hand, to share, still warm, with friends on the sofa.

Jambalaya

This is my friend Jen's jambalaya, which started life as Ina Garten's. It's blissfully easy to make, and keeps well in the fridge for a couple of days. The prawns get a bit rubbery on reheating so share them all out in the first serving, and then add a handful of fresh ones if you have any leftovers to warm up later. This is a great dish to make even if you're not feeding a crowd – offering comfort to either a group, or the solo sofa-diner.

Serves 6

1. Heat the butter in a heavy-bottomed lidded pan. Add the sausage and fry gently for about 8 minutes. Set aside. Add the celery, and onions, and fry in the fat from the sausages and butter until the onions are translucent. Stir the peppers through. Add the garlic, oregano, thyme, bay leaf, cayenne, and stir well. Cook for a couple of minutes, until fragrant.

2. Add the tomatoes and stock, stir, then bring to a boil. Return the sausage to the pan, and add the rice and hot sauce. Return to the boil and then reduce to a simmer over a gentle heat. Put the lid on and cook for 20 minutes. Stir occasionally to avoid the rice sticking.

3. Slice the prawns down their backs, and remove the vein. Add half the spring onions, half the parsley, the raw prawns, and a squeeze of lemon to the pot. Stir well. Put the lid on and turn off the heat. The prawns will cook in the residual heat; just leave it for 10 minutes before serving.

4. Taste, and season with salt and pepper. Garnish with the remaining spring onions and parsley and bring the hot sauce to the table for people to add themselves.

1tbsp butter
400g/14oz andouille or Polish sausage, sliced (if you can't get hold of these, use chorizo)
2 stalks of celery, diced
2 medium onions, diced
2 red/bell peppers, diced
2 cloves garlic, minced
1tsp dried oregano
1tsp chopped thyme leaves
1 bay leaf
2tsp cayenne pepper
1 x 400g/14oz tin chopped tomatoes
850ml/3½ cups chicken or ham stock*
2tbsp dark brown sugar**
250g/1⅓ cups long-grain rice
3–4 dashes of hot sauce (I use Frank's Hot Sauce)
300g/10oz raw peeled prawns/shrimp
2 spring onions/ scallions, finely sliced
A few sprigs of parsley, roughly chopped
A squeeze of lemon
Salt and black pepper

*Chicken stock is fine here, but the best jambalaya I've ever made was done with the cooking liquor leftover from Nigella's Coca-Cola ham. I obviously can't recommend you spend 2 hours simmering a ham in full-fat Coke just for this recipe, but if you do have the urge, it's a dream.
**Only add this if you're using chicken stock.

Macaroni cheese

I'm hard pressed to imagine a dish more comforting than this one; both to prepare, and to eat. I've made it on countless nannying nights, the day before a big school test, or on quiet, cold nights in when the kids would make a request for it.

Serves 4

1. Preheat your oven to 200C fan/425F/gas 7. Warm a frying pan over a medium heat and tip in the pancetta. Fry gently for around 15 minutes, stirring occasionally, while you get on with the rest of the dish. Don't add any butter or oil – the fat will come from the pancetta.

2. Cook the macaroni in boiling salted water until tender but with a little bite – around 7 minutes. Scoop out a mugful of the cooking water, then drain the pasta and set aside.

3. Melt the butter in a saucepan and, once it is bubbling, tip in the flour. Stir with a wooden spoon for 3 minutes to cook off the taste of the flour. Pour in the milk and whisk until the sauce thickens. Don't worry if this takes a couple of minutes; it will happen very suddenly, so do keep an eye on it and keep whisking, or it will become lumpy.

4. Over a very low heat, whisk in the Cheddar, mozzarella and cottage cheese until they melt and the sauce becomes stringy. Remove from the heat and add the nutmeg.

5. Tip the pasta and pancetta (and its fat) into the cheese sauce, lubricate it all with a splash of the cooking water, and stir well. Scoop the whole gooey lot into a greased ovenproof dish.

6. Top with breadcrumbs and grated Parmesan and bake for 20 minutes, until the cheese sauce is bubbling and the dish is browned in patches on top. Take it out of the oven and rest it while you sort out a salad or drinks before bringing the dish to the table.

125g/scant 1 cup diced pancetta or unsmoked lardons
250g/2¼ cups dried macaroni
50g/3½tbsp butter
50g/heaped ⅓ cup plain/all-purpose flour
300ml/1¼ cups milk
50g/½ cup mature/sharp Cheddar, grated
75g/⅔ cup mozzarella, grated
50g/¼ cup cottage cheese
A generous grating of nutmeg
2tbsp breadcrumbs
1tbsp grated Parmesan cheese

Peanut and smoked salt brownies

50g/⅓ cup peanuts (try to get unsalted ones)
300g/10oz dark/bittersweet chocolate
250g/1 cup + 2tbsp butter
150g/¾ cup light brown sugar
150g/¾ cup golden caster/superfine sugar
4 eggs
70g/½ cup plain/all-purpose flour
50g/½ cup cocoa powder
½tsp baking powder
A generous pinch of smoked sea salt

EQUIPMENT
25cm/10in square cake tin/pan

These are my all-time favourite brownies. They're dark and fudgy and rich and salty – everything I look for when I crave comfort. You can replace the peanuts with any nut you fancy, but there's something pleasingly American about this combination. In *A Confederacy of Dunces*, Ignatius J. Reilly's mother Irene sits with a box of brownies at the bar. Offering them to the bartender, she assures him 'they nice'. Ignore this faint praise – these are better than nice.

Serves 12–16

1. Preheat your oven to 150C fan/325F/gas 3. Butter and line the tin with parchment paper; the brownie will be too delicate to 'turn out', so do make sure you have plenty of paper to grasp hold of once it's baked.

2. Toast the peanuts in a dry frying pan over a low heat until golden brown, then set aside to cool. Bring a saucepan of water to a gentle simmer, and melt 200g/7oz of the chocolate in a heatproof bowl over it.

3. Put the butter and sugars into a bowl and beat until light and creamy – the sugar should no longer feel grainy between your fingers. Try to use an electric implement (electric hand whisk or stand mixer) if you have one, so you can get the mixture really light; if you don't have one, do beat for longer than you normally would.

4. Crack the eggs, one at a time, into the creamed butter and sugar, beating well after each addition. Pour in the melted chocolate, then chop the other 100g/3½oz of chocolate, and mix this through. Roughly chop the peanuts, and fold them through. Sieve the flour, cocoa, and baking powder into the mixture and fold in with a spatula until just combined. Do this gently, but make sure you get rid of any white streaks.

5. Pour the mixture into the tin, then smooth out the top. Place the batter in the oven for 40 minutes. After this time,

the batter will have risen a little and should have flaked on top. Remove from the oven when a skewer inserted comes out sticky, but without raw dough on it. Start checking the brownies after around 30 minutes, and err on the side of caution; you can always pop it back in for a minute or so, but you can't reclaim the dense fudginess the middle of a brownie should have. Sprinkle with the smoked salt, and leave to cool in the tin before cutting into squares.

Pancake day

My mother was too busy with Rosie to make pancakes, so I had a go. I don't know why my father went so mad, the kitchen ceiling needed decorating anyway.
The Growing Pains of Adrian Mole, Sue Townsend

It's been years since I gave up something for Lent. At my Catholic school, though, it was the done thing, and so I forewent chocolate, sweets, and being deliberately contrary in interactions with my sister (that one never lasted long). We were taught about Shrove Tuesday, and the tradition of using up perishable foods before the annual fast began, then we'd queue up at the tuck shop for a plate of pikelets, drizzled with honey, and served with a big spoonful of jam. We'd eat them with our hands, fingers sticky with the sugar, and bid farewell to sweet treats for the long weeks to come.

Of course, pancakes have been around for much longer than Shrove Tuesday. There's evidence that our prehistoric ancestors were eating something akin to a pancake in the Stone Age, they were enjoyed with honey by the Ancient Greeks and Romans, and the Elizabethans flavoured theirs with spices and rosewater. Pancakes are now made all over the world, from all types of starches and grains, and because of this familiarity they function as shorthand for domesticity. When lying to the police about a 'normal' morning at home, *The Goldfinch*'s Theo claims to have eaten a batch studded with blueberries and chocolate chips. Adrian Mole is cross every Shrove Tuesday at his mother's disinclination to make pancakes for the family. Pippi Longstocking welcomes her friends with a batch, and *Gone Girl*'s Amy makes some in an attempt to cast herself as a wholly domestic woman.

Despite my disinclination to take anything off the table during the lead-up to Easter, I still look forward to Pancake Day. My tastes have changed since childhood – I'm now more likely to make soured buckwheat pancakes, or potato ones seasoned with herbs, as I am sweet, fluffy pikelets – but there's something wonderfully ritualistic about making them: whisking the egg into the flour, adding the milk drop by drop, swirling the butter around the pan, and then eating the first one (an inevitable aesthetic failure) as you cook the second.

Ricotta pancakes with roasted rhubarb

I eat a lot of rhubarb during spring – in England, the beautifully vibrant stems appear on the shelves and in markets in late winter, heralding the arrival of the warmer months. These light, sweet, zingy pancakes are a dream companion.

Serves 2

1. Preheat the oven to 180C fan/400F/gas 6. Slice the rhubarb into 4cm/1½in pieces and place in a single layer in a roasting dish. Sprinkle with the sugar and clementine zest and squeeze the clementine juice over the top. Cover with foil, and roast for 15 minutes. Remove the foil, and roast for a final 5 minutes.

2. To make the pancakes, mix the ricotta, milk, egg yolk, clementine zest and juice together in a bowl. Fold through the flour, salt, and the baking powder.

3. Beat the egg white to stiff peaks. Loosen the pancake batter by stirring a third of it through, then gently fold in the rest.

4. Warm half a teaspoon of butter in a frying pan, then drop in dollops of the batter (a generous tablespoon is a pretty good measure). Cook until you see bubbles on top, then flip the pancake over, and cook for a minute on the other side until golden brown.

5. Serve the pancakes with the rhubarb, and a spoonful of yoghurt or sour cream, if you like.

RHUBARB
500g/1lb 2oz rhubarb*
2tbsp dark brown sugar
Zest and juice of 1 clementine

PANCAKES
150g/⅔ cup ricotta
50ml/3½tbsp milk
1 egg yolk
Zest and juice of 1 clementine
60g/scant ½ cup plain/all-purpose flour
A pinch of salt
½tsp baking powder
1 egg white
Butter, for frying

* You'll have more rhubarb than you need here, but I want to make sure it's worth turning your oven on for roasting it. Eat leftovers with muesli, on toast with any ricotta you have left, alongside pieces of grilled mackerel, or on meringues with some softly whipped cream.

Blueberry and cardamom Dutch baby

10 cardamom pods
3 eggs
50g/heaped ⅓ cup icing/confectioner's sugar
100g/¾ cup plain/all-purpose flour
A pinch of salt
150ml/⅔ cup milk
30g/2 tbsp butter
100g/¾ cup frozen blueberries (or fresh if you fancy making this in summer)

EQUIPMENT
An ovenproof frying pan/skillet or dish

These huge, puffed pancakes hail from America – from the Pennsylvania Dutch. They take a little longer to cook than ones done on the hob, but will feed a few of you, with no need to stand over a frying pan with a spatula. On sluggish weekend mornings, this has a definite appeal.

Serves 6

1. Preheat the oven to 220C fan/475F/gas 9. Place your pan in the oven to warm up. Open the cardamom pods, and bash the seeds to a powder.

2. Whisk the eggs and sugar in a bowl, then fold in the flour, cardamom, and salt. Whisk in the milk in stages, being careful not to overmix, or the batter will be tough.

3. Open the oven door, and put the butter in the pan. Close the door and leave it for a minute to melt. Pour the batter into the pan (be careful not to burn yourself!), throw in the blueberries, and then close the door quickly.

4. Bake the pancake for 18 minutes until puffed, crisp, and golden brown. Try not to open the door to check too often – wait at least 15 minutes before taking a peek. Dust with icing sugar and serve with a little sour cream.

The first signs of spring

68

Potato and thyme pancakes with hot smoked trout

I started making these pancakes as a vessel for leftover mashed potato, but I've recently taken to making them from just-cooked potatoes, which gives them a wonderful lightness. If you want to make them from scratch, three medium mashing potatoes (Maris Pipers are good) should give you enough potato to be getting on with.

Serves 4

1. To make the batter, sprinkle the flour, salt, and baking powder over the mashed potato. Whisk together the eggs, milk, and thyme leaves. Pour over the potato mix, and stir to combine.

2. Pop a small saucepan of water on to boil for the eggs.

3. Melt half the butter in a frying pan, and add half the vegetable oil. Spoon dollops of the batter into the pan, and fry over a low heat until bubbles are popping on the surface. Flip them over, and give them a minute. Keep them warm in a low oven until you've cooked all of the batter; add more butter and oil to the pan when needed.

4. While your pancakes are cooking, gently lower the 4 eggs into the pan of simmering water, and cook for 6 minutes. Run under cold water, crack the shells all over, and then peel them off. Serve a stack of the pancakes with flakes of the trout, some more thyme leaves, and a lovely runny egg.

PANCAKES
250g/¾ cup mashed potato
80g/⅔ cup plain/all-purpose flour
A pinch of salt
1tsp baking powder
2 eggs
125ml/½ cup milk
6 sprigs lemon thyme
30g/2tbsp butter
1tbsp vegetable oil

WITH
2 fillets hot smoked trout
Fresh thyme leaves
4 eggs

Japan in bloom

In front of the large window leading onto the terrace was a jungle of plants growing in bowls, planters, and all kinds of pots. Looking around, I saw the whole house was filled with flowers; there were vases full of spring blossoms everywhere.
Kitchen, Banana Yoshimoto (translated by Megan Backus)

In the spring of 2018, my surrogate sister Anna and I travelled to Japan. We'd been discussing doing so for ages – with our shared love of sushi, and her box set of Studio Ghibli films, it was only a matter of time. We booked our trip knowing that we'd miss hanami, the Japanese custom of celebrating the impossibly short cherry blossom season, by a matter of weeks. But we reasoned that we'd return another time to see the trees in all their brief glory.

We had a list of hundreds of things we wanted to do. An early morning visit to the Tsukiji fish market to watch the auction, and eat bowls of raw fish. An afternoon at the Studio Ghibli museum, taking in the carefully curated exhibitions. A cooking class in the home of a trained chef, who would demonstrate the process of making a perfect tamagoyaki (a Japanese omelette), before politely watching our attempts to mimic her. Endless bowls of various kinds of noodles, to be eaten in tiny hole-in-the-wall restaurants. A day of drinking coffee, eating pastry, and wandering along the canals, popping into every bookshop we passed.

In preparation, I buried myself in my books: I stood in the *Kitchen* alongside Mikage, Yuichi, and Eriko; discovered post-war Japan, and the changing role of women, in Kazuo Ishiguro's *An Artist of the Floating World*; and joined Mari Asai on a single night in Tokyo in Haruki Murakami's *After Dark*. Finally, after a couple of months spent surviving the Australian summer, I arrived in Tokyo just as winter was ending. On the first day, waiting for Anna to arrive, I ate nigiri and noodles, drank copious amounts of tea, and walked through the parks, listening to audiobooks. Expecting to see bare branches awaiting the celebrated blossom, I was overcome to realise that we'd arrived just as the plum blossoms had – the trees were a glorious shade of pink against the pale grey sky. We'd arrived to see Tokyo in spring, and it was an unmitigated joy.

Salmon bowl

Years ago, on the hunt for a simple supper, I came across Nigella Lawson's mirin glazed salmon. I still make a version of it with alarming regularity, and serve it alongside any other bits and pieces I have in the fridge. It's one of my most reliable standby suppers.

Serves 2

1. Rinse the rice a couple of times in cold water, and then cover with water and set aside to soak for 30 minutes.

2. Peel the carrot, and then cut into ribbons using a vegetable peeler. Add the salt and sugar to the vinegar, and stir to dissolve. Toss the carrot in the vinegar, and then set aside to pickle while you prepare the rest of the dish.

3. Drain the rice and place in a saucepan, add 120ml/½ cup water, cover with a lid, and bring to the boil. Reduce the heat to a gentle simmer and cook for 6–8 minutes, until the water dips below the level of the rice. Turn off the heat but keep the pan covered, and steam for 10 minutes. Fluff the rice with some chopsticks, and stir the mirin through.

4. For the salmon, mix the soya sauce, mirin, and sugar together in a bowl, then marinate the fish in it for a couple of minutes on each side. Fry the fish in a dry pan skin-side down over a moderate heat for 3 minutes. Flip the fish over, add the marinating liquid, and cook on the other side for a further 2 minutes. Remove the fish, then add the rice vinegar to the marinade, stir, and keep warm.

5. Lower the egg into a pan of boiling water for 6 minutes and then run under cold water. Peel and slice in half.

6. Flake the fish, and sprinkle the carrot with black sesame seeds.

7. Divide the rice between 2 bowls, add the salmon, along with a splash of the sticky sauce from the pan, and then the carrot, cucumber, egg, spring onion, pickled ginger, and a pinch of togarashi.

RICE
100g/½ cup sushi rice
2tsp mirin

QUICK PICKLED CARROT
1 carrot
A pinch of flaky sea salt
A pinch of sugar
1tsp rice wine vinegar
1tsp black sesame seeds

SALMON
2tbsp soya sauce
2tbsp mirin
1tsp dark brown sugar
2 salmon fillets (descaled, but with their skin still on)
1tbsp rice vinegar

AND
1 egg
½ cucumber, finely sliced
1 spring onion/scallion, finely sliced
Pickled ginger
Togarashi

Vegetable tempura and miso mayonnaise

MAYONNAISE
2 egg yolks
1tsp rice vinegar
300ml/1¼ cups
groundnut oil
2tbsp miso paste
Salt and white pepper

BATTER
2 litres/8½ cups
vegetable oil
1 egg
200ml/generous ¾ cup
fizzy water
125g/scant 1 cup plain/
all-purpose flour

VEGETABLES
Baby carrots, sliced in
half lengthways
Asparagus, sliced in half
Tenderstem broccoli,
base trimmed off
Spring onions/scallions,
sliced into batons
Radishes, sliced in half
lengthways, leaves still
attached

I ate a significant amount of tempura in Japan. It came atop noodles, piled up on plates alongside salt and matcha powder, or wrapped in rice and seaweed. I've always loved it with prawns, but the sheer variety of vegetables in tempura was fantastic. I came home determined to make it a frequent dinner party dish, using the first of the beautiful spring produce.

Serves 4

1. To make the mayonnaise, whisk the egg yolks in a bowl with the vinegar, and then pour in the oil in a slow stream, whisking constantly. To prevent it splitting, keep an eye on the oil, and go slow, adding more only when everything in the bowl has been incorporated. Stop once your whisk leaves visible streaks in the mayonnaise as you drag it through.

2. Strain the miso paste to remove any lumps, and then whisk it into the mayonnaise. Taste, and then season with salt and pepper.

3. For the tempura, pour the oil into a large, high-sided saucepan, and place over a moderate heat. Whisk the egg and fizzy water together in a jug. Pour the liquid over the flour, whisking constantly to prevent lumps forming. Place in the fridge until the oil is ready for frying.

4. Once the oil is at 180C/356F (or when a wooden spoon handle inserted into the oil has a family of bubbles fizzing around it), it's ready for frying. Dip the veg in the batter, and then place carefully into the hot oil. Fry until golden, then remove with a slotted spoon and drain on some paper towels, while you cook the next batch. Season with salt, and serve with the mayonnaise.

Chicken and spring onion yakitori

CHICKEN
6 boneless chicken thighs
6 spring onions/ scallions

SAUCE
200ml/generous ¾ cup soy sauce
100ml/scant ½ cup mirin
50g/¼ cup dark brown sugar
A thumb-sized piece of ginger, peeled and sliced into discs
100ml/scant ½ cup water (or sake, if you have it)
2tbsp cornflour/ cornstarch

AND
3tbsp sesame seeds

EQUIPMENT
8 skewers (metal, or wooden ones you have soaked for an hour or two)

There are a thousand tiny restaurants in Tokyo, just big enough to shuffle through. Whenever I wasn't eating inside one, I would stand on the street and watch the careful work of the chefs: noodles being pulled by hand, rice being formed for nigiri with extraordinary speed, and yakitori being deftly turned as it cooked over hot coals. On my final day, I ventured into the crowded yakitori place near our flat, and ate plate after plate of these delicious, sticky skewers.

Serves 4

1. First, prepare the chicken. You can make this with or without the skin (the fatty skin renders beautifully under the grill if you cook it for long enough, so I really like it with). Slice the meat into strips. Peel the outer leaves from the spring onions and cut them into chunks.

2. Thread the chicken and spring onions onto the skewers, alternating between the two, folding the chicken pieces in half (skin-side out), and pushing the skewer through both halves so that they are secured.

3. Set aside and prepare the sauce. Put the soya, mirin, sugar, ginger, and 50ml/3½tbsp of the water in a small pan, and bring to a gentle simmer. Whisk the cornflour in a small bowl with the rest of the water, then whisk it into the simmering liquid. Continue to cook the sauce until it is thick enough to coat the back of a spoon.

4. Heat the grill/broiler in your oven as hot as it will go. Put a piece of foil under a rack, and position it in the top section of the oven.

5. Place the skewers on the rack, and paint with the sauce. Cook under the grill for a couple of minutes, and then turn them over, and paint the other side. Keep flipping and painting them every couple of minutes, until the chicken is cooked through (about 15 minutes). Place the skewers on a serving plate, paint them one final time, and sprinkle with sesame seeds. Serve with rice or noodles.

Breakfasts in bed

Robert, this morning, complains of insufficient breakfast. Cannot feel that porridge, scrambled eggs, toast, marmalade, scones, brown bread, and coffee give adequate grounds for this, but admit that porridge is slightly burnt. How impossible ever to encounter burnt porridge without vivid recollections of Jane Eyre at Lowood School, say I parenthetically. This literary allusion not a success.
Diary of a Provincial Lady, E. M. Delafield

I look forward to no other meal quite so much as I look forward to breakfast. As I drift off to sleep, I often find myself imagining what I'll make the next morning; will it be a day for Vegemite soldiers and an egg, or a chance to turn the leftover roasted broccoli into something exciting? When I worked in an office, breakfast was a rushed affair – a banana or a bowl of porridge, and then a coffee once I arrived at work. But weekend mornings were sacred: a chance to luxuriate over the crossword, to progress from coffee to coffee (and eventually to tea), and to slip back beneath a blanket with a book.

When I was young, I couldn't imagine anything more grown up than eating breakfast in bed. Despite my promises to wash all the linen myself, my mum could read me like a book, and I was (quite rightly, given how clumsy I am) never permitted to climb beneath the sheets with a plate in my hand. On Mother's Day each year, my sister and I would plan a breakfast in bed for mum, brought to her on a folding tray. She patiently ate what we'd brought, but I suspect she was itching to be up and about, making something herself. She is famous for her breakfasts; the one she made after my eighteenth birthday party saw the ten or so of my pals who had slept on various sofas or patches of carpet stay for another 24 hours, in hopes of getting another one.

My favourite part of being freelance is that I can now treat every morning like a weekend. I write late into the evenings, long after everyone else has gone to bed, and so on glorious mornings in early spring, I can take my breakfast to the table outside, and sit with a book. Though there are fewer breakfasts in bed than I imagined adulthood would bring (they appeal a little less now that it really is me washing the linen), the breakfasts are better than I could have hoped for.

Everything in the fridge frittata

300g/10oz small, waxy potatoes
1tbsp groundnut oil
10 stalks Tenderstem broccoli
50g/1½ cups chopped kale
20g/¾ cup chopped parsley
6 eggs
90ml/⅓ cup double/heavy cream
100g/1 cup grated Cheddar
Salt and black pepper
50g/heaped ¼ cup ricotta

This is one of my favourite Sunday morning breakfasts; a brilliant way to use up any last bits in the vegetable drawer or cheese box at the end of the week. This version below is my favourite, but you can add anything you like. Season it generously, add whatever herbs you fancy, and take big slices of it outside to enjoy with the paper and some coffee.

Serves 6, or 2 with lunchbox leftovers

1. Preheat the oven to 200C fan/425F/gas 7. Boil the potatoes in salted water for about 10 minutes, until just tender. Meanwhile, warm the groundnut oil in a cast iron pan, or one without a plastic or wooden handle, that can be put directly into the oven, then add the broccoli and kale. Toss occasionally until browned.

2. Add the parsley to the vegetables, and toss it through. Drain the potatoes, and add them too, slicing any larger ones into pieces.

3. Whisk together the eggs, cream, Cheddar, and seasoning. Pour over the vegetables, and turn off the heat. Spoon the ricotta on top of the egg mixture.

4. Transfer to the oven for 8 minutes, and then switch the oven to grill at a high temperature until the top of the frittata is golden brown. Remove, and allow to cool for 5 minutes before serving.

French toast with salted caramel

SALTED CARAMEL
150g/¾ cup caster/
superfine sugar
120ml/½ cup double/
heavy cream
20g/1½tbsp butter
A large pinch of flaky
sea salt

FRENCH TOAST
3 eggs
30ml/2tbsp milk
A pinch of salt
30g/2tbsp butter
4 slices white bread

TO SERVE
Vanilla ice cream

The French toast eaten in Maria Semple's *Where'd You Go, Bernadette?* fulfils the craving of an expectant mother. She dreams of it sandwiching a large scoop of Molly Moon's salted caramel ice cream, but if you can't get to Molly Moon's in Seattle, vanilla ice cream and a big spoonful of salted caramel will provide a worthy substitute.* I use my friend Liv's salted caramel recipe, a jar of which is always somewhere in my kitchen, to satisfy any entirely non-pregnancy related cravings.

Serves 2

1. First, make the salted caramel. Melt the sugar to a rich, nutty brown in a pan, then take off the heat, and whisk in the double cream (it will bubble up, so watch your forearms). Whisk in the butter. Finally, season with a big pinch of flaky sea salt. Store it in a sterilized jar (see p. 158) in the fridge – it lasts about a month, but I guarantee you'll be eating it with a spoon before too long.

2. To make the French toast, use a fork to whisk the eggs in a wide dish, until there are no streaks of white or yolk. Add the milk and salt and whisk again.

3. Place a non-stick or cast-iron pan over a moderate heat, and put a tablespoon of the butter in the pan. Dip a piece of bread into the egg, and flip over to soak the other side too. Allow it to drip, and then place it into the foaming butter. Repeat with a second piece of bread. Once the bread is golden brown underneath, flip it over and cook on the other side. Add more butter, and then soak and fry the other 2 slices.

4. Serve with a scoop of ice cream, and a spoonful of salted caramel.

* I visited Molly Moon's a few years back. It's well worth a trip if you're in the area; I still think about their honey lavender, and that famous salted caramel.

Bloody Mary

If I fancy anything beyond coffee or tea in the morning, it's generally some form of a Bloody Mary. It's great with or without the gin and sherry; if I have tomato juice in my fridge, I'll drink a Virgin Mary with all the accoutrements, even if I don't want to add the booze.

Makes a jug for 6

1. Add all ingredients (except the lemon and celery) to a jug, along with a couple of handfuls of ice cubes. Stir to combine, and taste (in case you want more horseradish, Tabasco, or salt).

2. Pour into tall glasses and serve with a stick a of celery, a slice of lemon, and plenty of ice.

300ml/1¼ cups gin*
A thumb-sized piece of fresh horseradish, grated
1 litre/4¼ cups good tomato juice
1tsp Tabasco
1tbsp Worcestershire sauce
1tsp celery salt
Black pepper
60ml/¼ cup sherry (optional)

TO SERVE
1 lemon, cut into slices
Celery

* Traditionally, a Bloody Mary is made with vodka. I prefer gin with the sherry, but you can substitute vodka if you so wish.

Coffee butter and biscuits

BUTTER

50g/⅔ cup coffee beans
400ml/1¾ cups double/
heavy cream
100ml/scant ½ cup milk
A pinch of flaky sea salt

BISCUITS

125g/½ cup cold butter,
cubed
340g/scant 2 cups plain/
all-purpose flour
5g/1tsp fine salt
20g/2tbsp baking
powder
300ml/1¼ cups
buttermilk*
30g/2tbsp butter,
melted

EQUIPMENT

A piece of muslin/
cheesecloth, or a clean
dishcoth
Food processor

* You should have
this leftover from
making the butter; add
additional buttermilk,
or a couple of spoonfuls
of yoghurt if you need
more.

Shug Avery, ill in bed in Alice Walker's *The Color Purple*, is offered anything she wants for breakfast – ham, grits, biscuits, coffee, buttermilk, jam – but asks only for coffee. Celie sits beside her, 'lavishing' butter on a hot biscuit. The two women are yet to enter into the relationship that will change Celie's life, but it's a memorable breakfast nonetheless. It's a moment of calm, and an olive branch in the form of the biscuits that Shug falls upon as soon as Celie leaves the room.

Serves 4

1. To make the butter, put the coffee beans in a food processor and blitz for a second or two, to break them up a bit without turning them to a powder. Pour them into a bowl, add the cream, cover, and store in the fridge for 24 hours.

2. The next day, sieve the cream, leaving the beans behind. Pour the milk over the beans to loosen any stubborn cream, collecting this in the same bowl as the cream. Beat the milk and cream with an electric whisk or mixer, past stiff peaks, until the fat and liquid separate, and you are left with a clump of butter on the whisk, and buttermilk in the bowl.

3. Place a sieve lined with a clean piece of muslin over a bowl, and pour the buttermilk through it, collecting any small clumps of butter. Add the butter from the whisk, then mix through a pinch of flaky salt, and squeeze the muslin until it has stopped releasing buttermilk. Set the butter aside, and retain the buttermilk.

4. For the biscuits, preheat the oven to 220C fan/475F/gas 9. In a bowl, rub the cold butter (not the fancy coffee stuff, just the regular stuff) into the flour, salt, and baking powder with your fingertips, stopping just before everything is incorporated so the mixture still has flattened bits of butter running through it. Place in the freezer for 15 minutes.

5. Use a fork to mix the buttermilk into the flour and

butter, working quickly to bring the dough together. Flour your work surface, then roll the dough out into a rough rectangle. Fold this up like an A4 letter – a third over the middle third, and then the other third over the top. Turn the dough 90 degrees, roll out a little, and repeat the letter fold in the other direction.

6. Roll the dough out so it is an inch thick, then flour a fluted biscuit cutter (or a glass), and cut into 8 rounds, reshaping any offcuts and cutting through them again.

7. Place onto a lined baking sheet, brush the tops with melted butter, and bake for 12 minutes, until golden and well risen. Serve immediately with the coffee butter.

Capturing spring in a jar

Bathsheba resolved to hive the bees herself, if possible. She had dressed the hive with herbs and honey, fetched a ladder, brush, and crook, made herself impregnable with armour of leather gloves, straw hat, and large gauze veil—once green but now faded to snuff colour—and ascended a dozen rungs of the ladder.
Far From the Madding Crowd, Thomas Hardy

When the frost melts and flowers start to bloom, I set winter marmalades aside, and line my shelves with jars of honey in various golden shades. I start to think like *I Capture the Castle*'s Cassandra Mortmain: that there is nothing nicer to eat than the best bread, butter, and honey. I want honey that carries an imprint of the flowers and bees it came from: spicy, rich leatherwood honey; light, delicate orange blossom honey; dark, woody heather honey. I might spend most of my time in the Cotswolds valleys, but eating honey on a slice of toast enables me to travel: back to Australia, or to California, or to the Yorkshire moors.

I have recently been taken with the idea of bee-keeping, of preparing myself for the hives as Bathsheba does (though probably in slightly more modern clothing), of jarring the scent of the hills on which I live and storing it away – tracking the changes year by year. It's a hobby I fear would consume too much of my time and money and so, for now, I fear I must be satisfied with the work of other bee-keepers and their bees.

When I still lived in London, Hackney City Council planted a wildflower garden in London Fields. It sprang up almost overnight, when the days started to get longer and warmer, providing a welcome contrast from the usual burnt patches of grass where disposable barbeques had scorched the earth beneath them. As the season progressed, and the flowers bloomed, walking within a hundred metres of the garden was to breathe in the heady scent of honey. My top-floor flat was a short stroll away and, despite the pots of herbs I kept on the windowsill, it suffered for its lack of garden. And so, that spring, I spent weekend afternoons on a picnic blanket down in the park, lying on my back with a book, watching fat bumble bees flying against the breeze, buzzing gently towards the wildflowers.

Miso and honey roasted chicken

4 large chicken thighs, bone in, with skin
3tbsp red miso paste
3tbsp honey
2tbsp sesame oil
1 tbsp toasted sesame seeds

SLAW
1 carrot
5 radishes
A handful of kale leaves
¼ red cabbage
20g/1 cup coriander/cilantro leaves
20g/1 cup mint leaves
1 mild red chilli
1tbsp black sesame seeds

DRESSING
A thumb-sized piece of ginger
1tsp sesame oil
Juice of 1 lime
1tsp rice vinegar
1tsp honey
A pinch of salt

There is always a jar of miso paste somewhere in my fridge. I like it stirred through noodles, or painted onto scored aubergines before they're roasted, or whisked with a generous couple of spoonfuls of honey for this chicken. It makes a simple supper – just as good with the slaw as it would be with some noodles or rice, or some griddled Tenderstem broccoli.

Serves 4 for a light lunch, or 2 for dinner

1. Preheat the oven to 200C fan/425F/gas 7. Put the chicken thighs in a small roasting dish, making sure you don't leave too much space around them. Mix together the miso, honey, and sesame oil, and spoon it onto the chicken. Put the chicken thighs in the oven, and roast for 40 minutes.

2. While the chicken is in the oven, prepare the salad. Slice the carrot and radishes to a fine julienne (I have a julienne peeler I bought for a couple of quid that renders this the work of moments), and then slice the kale, cabbage, and herbs finely. Deseed the chilli and slice it finely, and add to the vegetables, along with the sesame seeds.

3. To make the dressing, grate the ginger, and whisk together with the other ingredients. Toss the dressing through the salad.

4. Check the chicken is cooked by inserting a skewer; the juices should run clear. Serve the chicken, sprinkled with the toasted sesame seeds, alongside a generous handful of the salad.

Baked Camembert with honey roasted nuts

If I add something to honey on buttered toast, more often than not it's cheese. Ricotta, sharp Cheddar, rich Stilton – I like pretty much all cheeses with a drizzle of honey. This is a fancier, dinner-party-friendly version: a lovely thing to linger over for a starter, or for dessert.

Serves 4 as a starter

1. Preheat the oven to 160C fan/350F/gas 4. Place the nuts in a single layer on a baking sheet, and transfer to the oven for 10 minutes until golden brown.

2. Meanwhile, melt the butter and honey in a saucepan over a low heat. Stir in the herbs, paprika, and salt. Pour this over the roasted nuts, mix through, and set aside.

3. Unwrap the Camembert, and place it back into the wooden box it came in, or on a sheet of parchment paper. Make some slashes in the top of the cheese, and push the garlic, rosemary sprigs, and thyme sprigs into it. Drizzle the honey over the top.

4. Seal the cheese inside the parchment paper, or place the wooden lid back over the top. Place on a baking sheet and bake for 20 minutes, until the centre is runny. Carefully transfer to a serving plate, making sure you don't get molten cheese on your hands, and serve with the nuts, some toast, and a handful of radishes.

NUTS
200g/1½ cups mixed unsalted nuts (almonds, walnuts, cashews, hazelnuts)
1tbsp butter
1tbsp honey
2 sprigs rosemary, finely chopped
2 sprigs thyme, finely chopped
½tsp smoked paprika
1tsp salt

CAMEMBERT
A whole Camembert (250g/9oz)
3 cloves garlic, peeled
2 sprigs rosemary
3 sprigs thyme
2tbsp honey

WITH
Slices of toasted sourdough
Radishes

Peanut butter, honey, and banana loaf

My favourite sandwich when I was at primary school was honey, peanut butter, and banana – Mum's sandwiches made mine the most creative (and undeniably the best) of all the school lunches in my class. This loaf is a slightly more grown-up version of my childhood favourite; a slice works in a lunchbox, for breakfast, or for morning tea. It's particularly good with coffee butter, if you find yourself with some leftover after eating the biscuits on p. 82.

Makes 10 slices

1. Preheat the oven to 160C fan/350F/gas 4. Grease and line a loaf tin. Melt the peanut butter, butter, sugar and honey in a saucepan. Allow to cool, then beat in the eggs. Peel and mash the bananas and then fold them in.

2. Stir in the flour, baking powder, nutmeg, and salt. Scrape into the tin, and bake for 50 minutes to an hour, until a skewer inserted in the cake comes out clean.

3. When the loaf comes out of the oven, rub the softened butter over the top. Cool for 10 minutes in the tin and then serve warm or toasted, with butter or ricotta, and a drizzle of honey.

60g/¼ cup crunchy peanut butter
60g/¼ cup butter
180g/scant 1 cup light brown sugar
100g/⅓ cup honey
2 eggs
3 large bananas, ideally quite brown*
150g/1 cup wholemeal flour
2tsp baking powder
½tsp freshly grated nutmeg
A pinch of salt
1tbsp butter, softened

* If your bananas are fresh and a pale, butter yellow, put them in the oven for half an hour or so while it heats up. They'll go brown, and will be perfect for this recipe. Don't forget to let them cool a little before peeling them open; they'll be impossibly hot inside.

Magical eggs

Dickon made the stimulating discovery that in the wood in the park outside the garden where Mary had first found him piping to the wild creatures there was a deep little hollow where you could build a sort of tiny oven with stones and roast potatoes and eggs in it. Roasted eggs were a previously unknown luxury and very hot potatoes with salt and fresh butter in them were fit for a woodland king—besides being deliciously satisfying.
The Secret Garden, Frances Hodgson Burnett

When I stayed with my friend Lean in Australia, I got to know her chickens. We visited the hutch every morning, letting them out so they could scratch around the garden, shake out their feathers, and peck indiscriminately at herbs. They left behind them a rainbow of pastel coloured eggs: a pale sky blue, a greenish teal, a dusky pink. Lean knows her chickens, and could tell me which egg came from which hen. Back in the kitchen, we boiled the eggs for breakfast, dipping generously buttered soldiers into the runny centres.

Humans have been eating birds' eggs for the entirety of recorded history, so it is of little surprise that we have discovered seemingly infinite ways to put them to use. Everyone has their favourite method of cooking them: I like them poached in quietly simmering water until the whites become opaque, fried in smoking hot oil so that the lacy edge of the white crisps up perfectly, or scrambled over the gentlest of flames until they can be spooned – still wobbling – onto toast. Dickon and Mary roast them under stones alongside tiny potatoes (make sure you poke a hole in the shell of your eggs if you want to try this, as they're liable to explode). *Call Me By Your Name*'s Oliver has to be shown the way of slicing the top off a boiled egg so he can dip toast into the yolk.

I marvel often at their utility, but it is when they are separated into yolks and whites that the true magic of eggs can be observed. The yolks can be employed to make rich hollandaise, velvety soft zabaglione, cured and grated as a seasoning, or cooked gently in milk and cream to make a custard thick enough to coat your tongue. The whites form the basis for meringue, feather-light cakes, or can be shaken with whisky, lemon, and ice to make a frothy cocktail. In short, there's nothing more useful in my kitchen than an egg.

Coddled eggs with anchovy toast

CODDLED EGGS
200g/¾ cup crème fraîche/sour cream
Salt and white pepper
¼tsp grated nutmeg
4 eggs

ANCHOVY TOAST
1 x 50g/1¾oz tin anchovies in olive oil
80g/⅓ cup butter
4 slices sourdough toast

TO SERVE
Chopped chives

EQUIPMENT
4 x 10cm/4in ramekins

This is the most warming and comforting egg-based meal I can imagine. Coddled eggs stay wonderfully wobbly in the middle, and the spiced crème fraîche that surrounds them is a thing of joy. The intensely savoury toast provides the perfect counterpoint, but there's no denying this is a rich dish that invites a little lie down afterwards – one to make on a lazy weekend, not when you have a busy day ahead of you.

Serves 4

1. Preheat the oven to 160C fan/350F/gas 4. Whisk the crème fraîche with the salt, pepper, and nutmeg, and divide half of it between 4 ramekins. Crack an egg into each ramekin, making sure the yolks do not break (you may like to crack each egg into a glass and then tip it into the pot to make sure). Cover with the rest of the crème fraîche.

2. Put the ramekins in a baking dish, place in the oven, and then fill the dish with warm water, trying not to splash any into the eggs. Bake for 15 minutes, until the white of the egg has just set.

3. While the eggs are in the oven, prepare the toast. Blitz the anchovies and butter together in a small food processor, or with a hand blender. Spread a thick layer onto the toast, and cut into soldiers.

4. Once out of the oven, top the eggs with chives, and serve immediately with anchovy soldiers for dipping.

Rösti Florentine

I spent years scared of hollandaise. It would split, or refuse to thicken, and I grew furious at the wasted ingredients. Then, finally, I cracked it. While a friend stood beside me, patiently adding butter, Julia Child coached me through, and I produced a thick, stable, delicious sauce. The trick? If it starts to look grainy, put a new egg yolk and a splash of lemon juice in a clean bowl. Add the split sauce a dribble at a time and watch it emulsify in the new yolk – like magic.

Serves 4

1. For the rösti, squeeze the potato and shallots in a clean tea towel to remove excess water. Season. Warm the butter and oil in a small frying pan over a moderate heat. Add the potato mix, flattening it down into the fat. Cook for 5 minutes, then flip over and cook for a further 4 minutes.

2. For the hollandaise, fill a small heatproof bowl with hot water. Allow it to sit for a minute, then tip the water into a small saucepan and bring it to a simmer. Dry the warmed bowl, add the egg yolks and lemon juice, and whisk.

3. Place the bowl over the pan of simmering water, ensuring the water does not touch the bottom of the bowl. Whisking continuously, add the butter, a little at a time. Only add more once the previous batch has been completely incorporated. Keep going, until you have a rich, thick sauce. Season to taste with salt, pepper, and mustard.

4. Wash the spinach, and wilt in a frying pan over a moderate heat. Add the butter, and season with salt.

5. Now poach your eggs. Bring a wide pan of water to a simmer. Crack an egg into a mug, swirl the water to create a whirlpool, lower the mug to the water, and drop the egg in. If the white spreads out, nudge it back towards the centre with a spoon. Repeat with the other eggs. Once the whites are cooked but the yolks are still runny (about 2 minutes), remove the eggs with a slotted spoon. Serve each egg with a quarter of the rösti, some spinach, and a generous spoonful of hollandaise.

RÖSTI
3 waxy potatoes, grated
2 banana shallots, finely sliced
Salt and black pepper
2tbsp butter
1tbsp groundnut oil

HOLLANDAISE
2 egg yolks
1tbsp lemon juice
125g/½ cup butter, very soft
Salt and black pepper
1tsp Dijon mustard

AND
200g/4 cups baby spinach
1tbsp butter
A pinch of salt
4 eggs

Lemon and lime meringue pie

PASTRY
200g/1½ cups plain/
all-purpose flour
2tbsp icing/
confectioner's sugar
A pinch of salt
125g/½ cup cold butter,
cubed
2tbsp ice-cold water

FILLING
Zest of 3 lemons and 3
limes
200ml/generous ¾ cup
citrus juice (from about
3 lemons and 3 limes)
60g/½ cup cornflour/
cornstarch
75ml/5tbsp cold water
200g/1 cup caster/
superfine sugar
5 egg yolks
100g/7tbsp butter

MERINGUE
300g/1½ cups caster/
superfine sugar
5 egg whites
1tsp cream of tartar

EQUIPMENT
Food processor
20cm/8in loose-
bottomed tart tin/pan
(round or long)

This is a delight of a dessert – a properly impressive dish to put into the middle of the table. You can use just lemons, if you prefer, but I like the bitterness of the lime alongside the sour lemon and pillowy, sweet meringue.

Serves 8

1. Preheat the oven to 180C fan/400F/gas 6. Put the flour, icing sugar, and salt in the bowl of a food processor. Add the butter and blitz until the mixture resembles breadcrumbs. Dribble in the water until the pastry comes together. Wrap in plastic wrap and chill for half an hour.

2. Roll the pastry out (you may need to do this between 2 sheets of parchment paper) and push it into a loose-bottomed tart tin. Chill for another half-hour.

3. Trim the pastry edges, line with a big sheet of plastic wrap, and pack with baking beans. Bake for 25 minutes, then remove the wrap and beans and bake for 10 minutes, until it's a rich, golden brown. Cool completely on a wire rack.

4. For the filling, mix together the zest, juice, cornflour, and water in a saucepan. Place over a very low heat and add the sugar and egg yolks. Whisk vigorously until smooth, then stir constantly until the mixture thickens and no longer tastes of cornflour. Remove from the heat and push through a fine sieve. Whisk in the butter. Once cool, spoon into the pastry shell and chill overnight, or for at least an hour.

5. When you're ready to serve, make the meringue. Wet the sugar with just enough water so that it feels like sand on the shoreline, and bring to a simmer. Boil until it reaches 115C/240F. Meanwhile, beat the egg whites until they form very soft peaks. On a medium speed, continue beating the egg whites while you pour in the hot sugar, then beat until cool. Fold through the cream of tartar.

6. Spoon or pipe the meringue onto the zesty filling, and brown with a blowtorch or under the grill. Serve in generous slices, cut through with a wet knife.

Zabaglione

This is kitchen magic – the sort of dish you won't be able to believe is made from only three ingredients. It's lovely to make at the end of a dinner party too – take your favourite guest into the kitchen with you to keep you occupied (or keep chatting with everyone, if your dining table is as close to the hob as mine is) while you whisk it up.

6 egg yolks
6tbsp golden caster/superfine sugar
4tbsp Marsala

Serves 6

1. Half fill a saucepan with water and bring it to the boil. Turn it down to a simmer, and keep it at this level while the zabaglione cooks.

2. Whisk the egg yolks and sugar together in a heatproof bowl until light and frothy. Add the Marsala, then place the bowl over the heat.

3. Whisk the mixture with an electric hand whisk on a medium speed for around 8 minutes (or by hand for up to 15 minutes, depending on your arm strength), until it has quadrupled in size. Ensure that the water doesn't boil too fiercely, and doesn't touch the base of the bowl at any point. Take off the heat.

4. Spoon into glasses and eat straight away, with Italian biscuits on the side for dipping into it, if you like.

More books for those months when the world is coming back to life...

As the frost melts in Milton, head out for a long, bracing walk with **North and South**'s Margaret Hale. Put a rabbit pie in the oven with **The Children who Lived in a Barn**. Journey across the Atlantic from Scandinavia with **The Emigrants**, and start to build a life in the new world. Hike up the mountains with **Heidi** and her grandfather, and keep warm with some fresh goats' milk and melted cheese on toast. Have a biscuit break with Juliet as she works on pages and pages of **Transcription**. Spend some time among the shelves with the **Convenience Store Woman**. Lust after Johnnie Ray with Penelope and Charlotte, and discover **The Lost Art of Keeping Secrets**. Track the culinary journey of **The Very Hungry Caterpillar**, from apples, through pizza, to some nice green leaves. Head to Paris and climb up through the attic windows to enjoy a picnic with the **Rooftoppers**. Spare a thought for **The Little Prince** as he carefully protects a single rose. Join Fern on a saunter around Zuckerberg's farm, and stop by the pigsty to read the words written into **Charlotte's Web**.

Spring in abundance

Spring in abundance

I enjoy the spring more than the autumn now. One does, I think,
as one gets older.
Jacob's Room, Virginia Woolf

Spring in Brisbane brought with it the jacaranda blossom that
carpeted the streets around our home in a pale purple-blue. It brought
frangipani flowers that we tucked behind our ears or into our braided
hair before school; bright white blooms, their centres streaked a
glorious butter yellow. It meant the arrival of the first mangoes of
the season, a return to the beach, where we dipped our toes into the
water, and a dusting off of the dining table on the deck, where we
started eating most of our meals. It meant school exams, and then the
fast-approaching holidays, and a packing away of all our cardigans and
school tights. It was the season during which I started to make plans
for summer excursions, and summer reading, and to pile up all the
novels I planned to devour once I was free from revision.

In England, it only feels as if spring has finally, properly arrived
when the wild garlic covers the hillsides and towpaths. Though the
possibility of a final cool, brisk day still hovers over us, once the garlic
is ready to be picked I start to embrace spring in earnest. This means
sleeping with the windows open, and being woken early by chirping
songbirds. It means crisp white sheets on the bed, and vases of brightly
coloured flowers on the dressing table. It means the first bloom of
elderflower, begging to be snipped from their stems and left to flavour
a bucketful of cordial. Spring means longer days, and time to linger
over meals eaten outdoors. It means savouring books about time spent
abroad in the sunshine, or about journeys into the English countryside
– stories that celebrate the abundance of green all around us. In late
spring, I love reading outdoors, enjoying the soft sunshine on my
shoulders as *Middlemarch*'s Dorothea finds herself falling in love with
Will. I re-join the Cazalet family, and my quiet longing to meet them
for Sunday lunch at Home Place. I bundle a picnic into a basket, follow
Sebastian and Charles into the grounds, and find a comfortable place
in the shade to revisit Brideshead.

I used to be a bit contrary about the arrival of spring; it meant the end of my favourite seasons, and the threat of summer on the horizon. But as I grow older, as Virginia Woolf suggested, I have found a lot to love in the green, generous richness of the season. I happily anticipate seeing the produce in the markets: asparagus piled high, bunches of crisp, peppery radishes, tiny little Jersey Royal potatoes, in need of a good scrub. I love those first few days of being unburdened of a just-in-case coat or jacket; of having everything I need in my pockets, and my hands free. I look forward to the increasingly longer evenings, to the scent of a load of laundered linen that has dried on the line outdoors over the course of an afternoon, to ice-cold bottles of beer in the garden as the sun sets. Spring, I am somewhat surprised to realize, is a joy.

A house in Italy

She jumped up, pulled on her slippers, for there was nothing on the stone floor but one small rug, ran to the window and threw open the shutters. 'Oh!' cried Mrs. Wilkins. All the radiance of April in Italy gathered together at her feet. The sun poured in on her.
The Enchanted April, Elizabeth von Arnim

On a cool May night in 2017, I slept against the wall of a Costa Coffee at Stansted airport. I'd been catering the first wedding of the season and, instead of collapsing into bed afterwards, the team had dropped me off at the terminal. Before the sun rose, I gathered my things and made my way through security. I was bound for Italy, and a long-planned reunion with my mum, stepdad, and granny (from Australia), sister and brother-in-law (from America), and my surrogate English family (from the Cotswolds) to celebrate some thirtieths, a sixtieth, and all of us being together.

What followed was a fortnight of superlative food and glorious weather. We visited local markets, and walked away laden with fresh spring vegetables and fruit. We took turns cooking in the terracotta-tiled kitchen, lay on the grass by the pool, and ate our meals at a long table in the garden. I read an impossibly large stack of books about British women falling in love with Italy: the house filled with not-quite friends in *The Enchanted April*, Lucy Honeychurch standing in a field of violets in *A Room with a View*, even *Middlemarch*'s Dorothea Brooke (Casaubon by then, sadly) on honeymoon in Rome. I understood how they felt – after months of cold, grey winter, the Italian sun warmed me to my bones.

I remember so much about that holiday, but there is one meal that will stay with me forever. We piled into the car one morning; Granny had suggested our destination, drawing on a decades-old memory of a restaurant that was almost certainly no longer there. We wandered the streets of a tiny hilltop village in Piedmont, and eventually found a vista she vaguely remembered. The restaurant was different (of course), but we went in regardless. We sipped on tonic and vermouth, ate local cheeses and delicious seafood, and finished the meal with a slice of tiramisu cake we all fell in love with. It was an entirely perfect day.

Broad bean crostini

400g/heaped 3⅓
cups podded broad/
fava beans, or around
1.5kg/3lb 5oz fresh
beans in their pods
Zest of 2 lemons
30g/1½ cups mint
leaves, chopped
60g/¾ cup pecorino
Salt and black pepper
8 slices ciabatta or
4 slices sourdough
60ml/¼ cup olive oil
150g/⅔ cup ricotta

There are few lovelier pairings than fresh, tender broad
beans and sharp, salty pecorino. This works beautifully as
a starter for a few of you, but I most frequently eat it for
brunch on Sundays in late spring, relishing the feeling of
splitting open the pods, and popping the beans out of their
skins, while Radio 4 plays in the kitchen.

Serves 4

1. Pod the broad beans into a sieve or colander. Give them
a rinse, and then place a lid over them and steam over a pan
of simmering water for 3 minutes.

2. If the beans are young (as they will be in late spring), you
won't need to skin them. If their skins are a little tougher,
break through them and pop the beans out into a bowl.
Let them cool to room temperature, and then add the
lemon zest, the mint, and shave in the pecorino. Toss it all
together and season with salt and pepper.

3. Brush the bread on both sides with olive oil. Place in
a warm frying pan, and cook until golden brown on one
side, then flip over and cook on the other side. Spread with
ricotta, top with the beans and pecorino, and drizzle with
a little more oil.

Sardines and bitter salad

Sardines are named for the island of Sardinia, where they were first found in plentiful shoals. They're simple to cook – they need only a couple of minutes over a hot barbeque or in a pan. When it's warm, I want little more than a sharp salad to accompany them.

Serves 4

1. Score the flesh of the sardines on each side with a couple of slashes of your knife. Squeeze the lemon juice over the fish, drizzle with olive oil, sprinkle with oregano, and season inside and out with salt and pepper. Allow to sit while you prepare the salad.

2. Whisk the lemon juice and garlic together in a large bowl, followed by the olive oil and season with salt and the oregano.

3. Wash the lettuces and radicchio. Dry with paper towels, and slice the core out of each of the leaves. Finely shred the lettuce, radicchio, parsley and mint. Toss through the dressing.

4. Warm a pan over a high heat until it is searingly hot. Lay the sardines in the pan, and cook for a few minutes until the skin is crisp and charred. Flip over, and cook on the other side for another couple of minutes. Serve hot, with the salad alongside.

SARDINES
12 fresh sardines, cleaned and gutted
Juice of 2 lemons
3tbsp olive oil
1tbsp dried oregano
Salt and black pepper

SALAD
2tsp lemon juice
2 cloves garlic, crushed
2tbsp olive oil
A pinch of salt
A pinch of dried oregano
2 Little Gem/Bibb lettuces
1 head radicchio
30g/1½ cups parsley leaves
30g/1½ cups mint leaves

Tiramisù alla nicciola della mamma (Hazelnut tiramisu cake)

My stepdad Geoff, never normally a fan of desserts, will rarely pass up a chance to order a tiramisu. And so, after the extraordinary lunch in Piedmont, though we all shook our heads at the idea of another course (tiramisù alla nicciola della mamma), he made sure there was some on the table for us all to share. What arrived was unlike any tiramisu I'd ever eaten. Lighter than we expected, served in an impressively tall slice, and without the familiar flavour of coffee, we fell upon it eagerly. I'm not sure Geoff even got a look-in. What follows is my mum's, and then my, attempts to recreate it at home. It's pretty close, and is now our favourite tiramisu-ish dessert.

Serves at least 10

1. First, make the sponge cake. Preheat the oven to 160C fan/350F/gas 4 and grease and line the sandwich tins with butter and parchment paper. Beat the eggs and sugar until thick, pale, and fluffy. When you lift the whisk, the batter should leave a trail behind. Sift in the flour and baking powder, and fold in gently. Pour the cool melted butter down the side of the bowl, and fold it in too.

2. Divide the batter between the cake tins, and bake for 25–30 minutes in the centre of the oven, until golden brown on top, and shrinking away from the side of the tins. Cool for 10 minutes in the tins, and then completely on a wire rack. Slice each in half horizontally.

3. Meanwhile, make the mousse for the top of the cake. Blitz the hazelnuts and a tablespoon of the sugar until they form a paste. Whisk together the egg yolks, 2 tablespoons of water, and 2 tablespoons of the sugar in a large bowl. Put the bowl over a pan of simmering water, ensuring that the base doesn't touch the water. Whisk over the heat until thick ribbons form when you lift the whisk, and the mixture is at 70C/158F. Cool slightly, then fold in the melted chocolate and the hazelnut paste.

SPONGE
8 eggs
250g/1¼ cups golden caster/superfine sugar
250g/1¾ cups + 2tbsp plain/all-purpose flour
3tsp baking powder
100g/7tbsp butter, melted and cooled
80ml/⅓ cup Marsala

MOUSSE
75g/½ cup hazelnuts, toasted and skinned
3 eggs, separated
5tbsp golden caster/superfine sugar
120g/4¼oz dark/bittersweet chocolate, melted
A pinch of salt
125ml/½ cup double/heavy cream

FILLING
500ml/2 cups double/heavy cream
250g/1 cup mascarpone
70ml/4½tbsp Marsala

EQUIPMENT
Food processor
2 x 20cm/8in sandwich tins/pans
20cm/8in loose-bottomed tin/pan

4. Beat the egg whites with a pinch of salt until soft peaks form. Bring the final 2 tablespoons of sugar to a simmer, along with 3 tablespoons of water. Boil until it reaches 105C/220F, then slowly add the hot syrup to the whites, beating until they form stiff peaks, and leave to cool.

5. Fold a third of the egg whites into the chocolate mixture to loosen it, and then gently fold in the rest. Beat the cream to soft peaks, and fold this in too. Keep the mousse in the fridge until you're ready to assemble the dessert.

6. To make the filling, beat the cream, mascarpone, and Marsala until light and creamy.

7. Line a cake tin with parchment paper to help the dessert come out more easily once it's assembled. Place one of the cakes into the tin, and splash a tablespoon of the Marsala onto it. Spread a third of the mascarpone filling onto the cake, and then top with another cake, more Marsala and mascarpone mix. Repeat again, then top with the final cake, the last of the Marsala, and then the hazelnut and chocolate mousse. Level out the top, cover with plastic wrap, and refrigerate for at least a couple of hours.

8. Remove from the fridge 10 minutes before serving, take out of the cake tin, throw some cocoa at the sides to decorate it if you like, and serve in slices.

Vermouth, tonic, and basil

150ml/⅔ cup Italian/
rosso vermouth
150ml/⅔ cup tonic
water
8 basil leaves
Ice cubes

As we sat down in that little hilltop restaurant, we were
offered an aperitivo (and some antipasti). I've been making
this drink ever since; fragrant and refreshing, it's perfect
for a spring afternoon in the garden.

Makes 4

1. Divide the vermouth and the tonic between 4 glasses.
Add a couple of basil leaves and a couple of ice cubes to
each. Serve.

Long Sunday lunches

For Sunday lunch they would have the roast lamb and summer
pudding. That settled, she was free to spend the morning in her
garden; dead-heading, clipping the four pyramids of box that were
stationed at the end of the herbaceous borders guarding the sundial
with Billy to sweep up and clear away the clippings.
The Light Years, Elizabeth Jane Howard

The Sunday roast is, deservedly, a British institution. As the
weekend draws to a close, pubs around the country fill up with
families and groups of friends ordering roast meat and veg, a
jug filled with rich gravy, and hoping (if they're anything like
me) for a Yorkshire pudding the size of their dinner plate. There
will be a box of Scrabble somewhere, higgledy-piggledy rooms,
something delicious on tap, and a beer garden to snaffle a table
in if the afternoon is fine. You need a pub like The Trout Inn, run
by Malcolm's parents in Pullman's *La Belle Sauvage*, where you
can settle into a cosy nook and eat a plate of 'endless, effortless,
generous food', taking comfort in its consistency and regularity.

This wouldn't be a bad way to spend a few hours each Sunday, but I
think my favourite roasts are the ones enjoyed at home, stretching
out on sofas once we've filled up on slow-cooked lamb or bowls of
crumble. And so, as the days grow longer, I find myself planning as
many weekend lunches as possible; inviting people to come round
in the early afternoon, and waving them all off again before the sun
sets in the evening. It's my favourite meal to host, especially as (if
I time it right) I can spend the evening with a book in an armchair,
knowing that all the washing up has already been done.

When I host these Sunday lunches, I do so with Elizabeth Jane
Howard's Cazalets in mind; I want to make a lunch that Mrs Cripps,
their cook, would approve of. I long to get lost in the garden at
Home Place: beds full of fresh, crisp vegetables; trees that hang
heavily with greengages; a thousand places to hide during an
hours-long game of hide and seek. I await an invitation to join the
Cazalets for lunch, so, in the meantime, I roast joints of meat, set
the table for as many as we have chairs for, and quiz everyone on
whether they're a Clary, a Louise, or a Polly (or a Rachel, a Villy, a
Zoe, or a Sybil).

Roasted shoulder of lamb with watercress, pea, and radish salad

This meal always goes down a storm. It's simple to prepare, and though the salad looks impressive, it is almost laughably easy. Serve the lamb warm, but well rested, and avoid the last minute scramble to get everything out hot. The Duchy and the rest of the Cazalets would be over the moon with it.

Serves 6

1. Preheat the oven to 150C fan/325F/gas 3. Place the lamb in a roasting tin, and make slashes into the fat. Spoon over the honey and rub it in. Pull the rosemary from the stalks, and sprinkle over the top. Pour over the oil and season with the salt. Roast in the oven for 4 hours.

2. Halve 10 of the radishes, and place in a small saucepan with the cider vinegar, salt and sugar. Bring to a simmer, turn off the heat, and leave to cool.

3. Take the lamb out of the oven, and leave to rest for 20 minutes. Pull the flesh apart with two forks (it should come away easily from the bone), and pile it up on a plate. If you're not ready to eat yet, the lamb can be warmed through in a low oven before serving.

4. To make the gravy, place the pan with the lamb juices over a low heat and, once simmering, whisk in the flour. Cook out for a couple of minutes, then add the stock, and simmer until thick. Add the mustard, then taste and season. Sieve, and keep warm.

5. Pick the watercress and mint leaves from their stems. Put the frozen peas in a sieve and run them under cold water to defrost. Thinly slice the uncooked radishes.

6. Make the dressing by whisking together the vinegar, mustard, and pepper, then whisk in the olive oil. Toss the watercress, mint, sliced radishes and peas in the dressing. Place on a plate and top with the pickled radishes, and the goat's cheese, torn into chunks. Serve alongside the lamb.

LAMB
2kg/4lb 8oz lamb shoulder (bone in)
4tbsp honey
3 sprigs rosemary
50ml/3½tbsp olive oil
2 tsp salt

GRAVY
2tbsp flour
200ml/generous ¾ cup vegetable stock
1tsp English mustard
Salt and black pepper

SALAD
15 radishes
100ml/scant ½ cup cider vinegar
A pinch of salt
1tsp granulated sugar
100g/2 cups watercress
30g/1½ cups mint leaves
300g/2½ cups frozen peas
120g/½ cup soft goat's cheese

DRESSING
1tbsp vinegar (reserve some after you pickle the radishes)
1tsp English mustard
Black pepper
1tbsp olive oil

Spiced pea falafel with pitta bread and hummus

FALAFEL
200g/1½ cups frozen peas, defrosted
1 x 400g/14oz tin chickpeas
1tsp ground coriander
1tsp ground cumin
2 cloves garlic
1tbsp tahini
2tbsp plain/all-purpose flour
1tsp baking powder
A pinch of salt
15g/¾ cup chopped parsley leaves
15g/¾ cup chopped mint leaves
1tbsp sesame seeds
1 litre/4¼ cups vegetable oil

PITTA
180g/1¼ cups plain/all-purpose flour
180g/1¼ cups strong bread flour
7g/2¼tsp easy-action yeast
A generous pinch of salt
250ml/1 cup lukewarm water

HUMMUS
1 x 400g/14oz tin chickpeas
3tbsp tahini
1 clove garlic
Juice of 2 lemons

AND
Courgette/zucchini pickle
Pickled red onions
Fresh coriander/cilantro
Yoghurt
Cherry tomatoes

EQUIPMENT
Food processor

This is an entirely different sort of Sunday lunch. It's brilliant fun to have on the table; hands on, and a little bit messy. There are a number of component parts but you can sub in shop-bought alternatives (the hummus, pitta and pickles could come ready-made if you prefer). That said, a Sunday morning spent putting this together may be right up your street – it is certainly up mine.

Serves 6

1. To make the falafel, blitz together the peas, chickpeas, spices, garlic, tahini, flour, baking powder, and salt in a food processor. Keep an eye on it; you want some texture to remain, so pulse your food processor rather than heading off to prep something else while you let it run.

2. Scoop the mix into a bowl, and add the chopped herbs and sesame seeds. Form into 18 balls, making sure you squash them together really well (they'll come apart in the oil if you don't). Set aside in the fridge for at least an hour while you make the pitta.

3. To make the bread, put the flours in a bowl, and add the yeast on one side and the salt on the other. Add the water and mix together by hand. Knead until the dough is smooth and elastic, and bounces back when prodded. Place in a clean bowl, cover with a tea towel, and leave to double in size (about an hour).

4. For super smooth hummus – if you can be bothered – first peel the chickpeas, then blitz them with the tahini, and garlic. Add the lemon juice and then some cold water to achieve a spreadable consistency. Taste and season.

5. Once the dough has risen, split it into 9 even pieces and shape into balls. Flour your surface, place the balls onto it, and cover with the tea towel again. Allow them to double in size (around 45 minutes). Once ready, the dough will bounce back when prodded.

6. Preheat the oven to 220C fan/475F/gas 9. Line two baking sheets with parchment paper. Roll each pitta into a circle about 5mm/½in thick. Place on the baking sheets, and bake for 7–9 minutes, until golden and puffed up. Wrap them in foil – this will keep them warm, but also soften them, making them easier to eat.

7. While the pittas are in the oven, fry the falafel. Pour the oil into a high-sided saucepan, and place over a moderate heat. When the oil is at 180C/355F (test with a thermometer, or the handle of a wooden spoon – a steady stream of bubbles will form around the handle when it is hot enough), drop in the falafel, and fry until crisp and golden brown. Scoop them out, and drain on paper towels.

8. Serve the falafel and hummus with coriander leaves, some yoghurt, and some cherry tomatoes, as well as the pickles. Put everything in the middle of the table, and allow people to stuff their own pitta.

Courgette pickle
Makes enough to fill a 750ml/25oz jar

1. Slice the courgette into thin ribbons – a vegetable peeler is the ideal tool. Sprinkle with the salt and allow to sit for an hour so that some of their moisture leaches out. Rinse in cold water.

2. Bring the vinegar, sugar, cumin and coriander seeds, and the chilli flakes to a simmer in a saucepan, stirring occasionally to ensure the sugar dissolves.

3. Push the courgette and shallots into the jar, and pour over the flavoured vinegar. Leave for at least a couple of hours before eating – it will keep for a couple of weeks.

Pickled red onion
Makes enough to fill a 400ml/14oz jar

1. Sprinkle the onions with salt and then squeeze with your hands until they start to soften.

2. Push into a jar, and cover with vinegar. They'll be ready to eat within half an hour, but will also last for a good few weeks.

COURGETTE PICKLE
2 large courgettes/ zucchini
1tbsp rock salt
500ml/2 cups cider vinegar
100g/½ cup caster/ superfine sugar
1tbsp cumin seeds
1tbsp coriander seeds
1tsp chilli flakes
2 banana shallots, sliced

PICKLED RED ONION
2 red onions, sliced
A generous pinch of flaky sea salt
250ml/1 cup cider vinegar

Roasted sea bass, green olives, spring couscous

2 x 1kg/2lb 4oz sea bass, scaled and gutted
Salt and black pepper
2 lemons
20g/¾ cup thyme sprigs
Stalks from a small bunch of dill
2tbsp olive oil
200g/1⅔ cups green Sicilian olives

COUSCOUS
250g/1½ cups couscous
250ml/1 cup weak vegetable stock
40g/2 cups wild garlic leaves
20g/1 cup mint leaves
20g/1 cup parsley leaves
Fronds from a small bunch of dill
A pinch of salt
2tbsp olive oil
2 spring onions/ scallions, finely sliced

EQUIPMENT
Blender or stab mixer

As Sunday roasts go, fish is one of my favourites. It cooks so quickly, allowing this whole meal to be on the table in around half an hour. The couscous started life as an Ottolenghi recipe, made even more fresh and spring-like thanks to the addition of wild garlic.

Serves 6

1. Preheat the oven to 200C fan/425F/gas 7. Make 3 deep slits in each side of the fish, and season inside and out. Cut the lemons into rounds, and place into the cavity of each fish. Push thyme and dill stalks in as well, and place in a roasting dish. Drizzle olive oil over the top, put the olives in around the fish, and transfer to the oven for 20 minutes.

2. Prepare the couscous. Pour the grains into a bowl, and pour the hot stock over the top. Cover with a tea towel, and leave for 10 minutes.

3. Blitz the herbs with the salt and olive oil in a small blender or with a stab mixer. Fluff the couscous with a fork, and then stir the herb mix through. Top with the spring onions, and serve warm or at room temperature alongside the fish.

Spring in abundance

Yorkshire puddings

If you're aiming for a classic Sunday lunch, you can't do better than putting a Yorkshire pudding on each plate. In Helene Hanff's glorious *84, Charing Cross Road*, she records years of correspondence with Frank Doel, who works in a bookshop at the eponymous address. At one point, Doel's wife Cecily sends Helene a recipe for Yorkshire pudding: 'a cup of flour, an egg, a half cup of milk and a good shake of salt' to be baked in the oven with the joint of meat. It's worth remembering that Cecily was writing during rationing, so her one egg feels a little meagre now. Regardless, Helene's review, that the Yorkshire puddings are 'out of this world', is entirely correct.

125g/1 cup - 1tbsp plain/all-purpose flour

3 eggs

200ml/generous ¾ cup milk

A pinch of salt

3tbsp beef dripping (or vegetable oil, if you prefer)

Makes 6

1. Tip the flour into a large bowl. Make a well in the centre, and crack in the eggs. Start to add the milk, whisking from the centre to slowly incorporate the flour, until it is the consistency of double/heavy cream. Season with salt, and rest the batter for at least an hour, or overnight if it makes your planning easier.

2. Preheat the oven to 230C fan/475F/gas 9. Place a muffin tray, or Yorkshire pudding pan, in the oven to heat up. After a couple of minutes, add a little of the fat to each hole on the tray, and heat in the oven for about 10 minutes.

3. Take the tray from the oven and, quickly but carefully, pour the batter into the holes. Bake for 15–20 minutes, until puffed and dark golden brown.

Easter feasting

At some point quite early on I forgot what the party was all about and began to enjoy myself. While Anouk played in Les Marauds, I orchestrated preparations for the largest and most lavish meal I had ever cooked, and became lost in succulent detail.
Chocolat, Joanne Harris

At Catholic school, the lead up to Easter was always a whirlwind of liturgies and masses, first-term examinations, playing Pontius Pilate in Good Friday re-enactments, and planning for the fast-approaching holidays. It was a busy time of year, and the time off was immensely welcome. My family's Easter rituals were not as set in stone as our Christmas ones – something about the dates changing from year to year always made it feel more fluid – but we'd generally have fish and chips on the Friday evening, and then a big lunch on the Sunday.

As I grew older, and left my link with the Church behind, Easter became an opportunity to spend a few days in the kitchen trying out complex baking, and reading books from cover to cover. Easter Sundays over the years have seen a procession of rabbit pies, roast chickens, legs of lamb, and whole brown crabs cracked open with a hammer in the absence of more appropriate tools. I have baked batches of hot cross buns, turning the leftovers into a sort of bread and butter pudding, and experimented with various recipes for lemon meringue pie (my favourite ended up on p. 96).

Cooking at Easter always makes me think of Vianne Rocher, chocolatier and renegade villager in *Chocolat*. Compared with her, my Easter excess seems positively miserly. Vianne's arrival in Lansquenet-sous-Tannes, just as Lent is beginning, scandalizes the local clergyman who attempts to set everyone against her. In the week before Easter, she prepares a remarkable feast for a friend's birthday, during which she serves her guests tomato soup with fresh basil, tarts filled with anchovies and tomatoes on 'biscuit-thin pâte brisée', vol-au-vents, elderflower sorbet, platters of seafood, chocolate fondue, and chocolate ice-cream with coffee, Calvados, and truffles. It's the sort of meal that would be near impossible to serve outside of a book, but in a story, it's perfect – an afternoon of excess at the end of the Lenten fast.

Spring in abundance

Tomato tart with capers and olives

PASTRY

200g/1½ cups plain/
all-purpose flour
100g/7tbsp butter
A pinch of salt
3tbsp cold water

FILLING

2 red onions, finely
sliced
1tbsp olive oil
3 cloves garlic, minced
1 x 400g/14oz tin
tomatoes, roughly
chopped
1tbsp red wine vinegar
1tbsp caster/superfine
sugar
Leaves from 6 sprigs
thyme
Salt and black pepper
2tbsp capers
8 anchovies
16 cherry tomatoes,
halved
24 pitted black olives
Juice of 1 lemon
Fresh basil leaves
Olive oil

EQUIPMENT

8 small loose-bottomed
fluted tart tins/pans (or
1 large)

These tarts are a wonderful home for the early season tomatoes, the ones that begin to smell like the promise of summer, but are helped by a little time spent in the oven. The tart below is an imagined version of one of the first courses enjoyed at Vianne's feast: tartelette méridionale, a southern tart that steals a little from a pissaladière, and a little from the flavours of a Provençal tapenade.

Makes 8

1. First, make the pastry. In a food processor, blitz together the flour, butter, and salt. You can also do this by hand, rubbing with your fingertips until the mixture resembles breadcrumbs. Add the water slowly; you need just enough to bring it together. Knead as little as possible, then wrap and chill for half an hour.

2. Separate the pastry into 8 equal pieces. Roll into balls, and then roll out to 3mm/⅛in thick discs. Place in the tart tins, and push into the corners. Chill for another half-hour.

3. Preheat the oven to 200C fan/425F/gas 7. For the filling, fry the onions in the oil for 10 minutes, until softened. Add the garlic and fry for a couple of minutes. Tip in the chopped tomatoes, and cook over a moderate heat until they've collapsed. Add the vinegar, sugar, and thyme. Cook until thick and not too wet. Taste and season. Turn off the heat and stir in the capers.

4. Once the pastry is chilled, trim the overhang. Prick the base all over with a fork, line each tart with plastic wrap, and fill with baking beans. Place on a baking sheet, and bake for 20 minutes. Remove the wrap and beans, and bake for a further 10 minutes, until golden and dry to the touch.

5. Divide the filling between the tart shells, and top each with an anchovy, 4 halves of cherry tomatoes, and 3 olives. Transfer to the oven for a final 15 minutes. Dress with a spritz of lemon juice, basil leaves and a drizzle of olive oil. Serve warm.

Plateau de fruits de mer

This recipe is basically an impressive assembly job. I make no apologies for this – there's no better way to eat a pile of seafood than simply with some lemon, bread, and mayonnaise.

Serves 8

1. If you buy your crabs live, put them in the freezer for 20 minutes. Remove, then place them on their backs. Lift the tail flap, and drive a skewer through the indent underneath, moving it quickly from side to side. Drop the crabs into a large pan of boiling salted water, and cook for 15 minutes.

2. Boil the prawns in plenty of salted water for 2–5 minutes. As soon as they turn pink, drain and set aside.

3. For the mayonnaise, whisk the egg yolks until thick. Whisk in the lemon juice and mustard. Very slowly add the oil, whisking continuously. Continue until you have used most of the oil and the mayonnaise is very thick. Season with the salt.

4. To prepare the crabs, turn them upside down. Place your thumbs under the base of the central piece of the shell and push up to remove the core. Discard the white gills, then pick out the white meat. Dig your thumb in behind the eyes, and lift out the bones. Discard them. Scoop out the brown meat, and mix it with some salt and lemon juice. Crack the legs and claws with a hammer, and pull the meat out, using a skewer to get into the crevices.

5. Just before you serve, open the oysters. Hold one firmly in a towel, with the flatter shell on top. Put an oyster knife or spoon into the hinge and wiggle to loosen. Run it along the shell, and then underneath the oyster to release. Flip the oyster over, and place the shell on a plate of ice.

6. Serve everything in the middle of the table, with finger bowls filled with chilled water and sliced lemon, some bread, plenty of serviettes, and wine.

THE FRUITS OF THE SEA

3 x 1kg/2lb 4oz brown crabs
500g/1lb 2oz raw prawns/shrimp, in their shells
16 oysters, in their shells
Ice cubes

MAYONNAISE

2 egg yolks
Juice of 1 lemon
1tsp Dijon mustard
250ml/1 cup groundnut oil
A pinch of salt

AND

Ice cubes
3 lemons
2 baguettes

Chocolate ice cream with coffee and Calvados

550ml/2¼ cups double/
heavy cream
250ml/1 cup milk
1tsp vanilla extract
A generous pinch of
flaky sea salt
8 egg yolks
100g/¾ cup icing/
confectioner's sugar
150g/5½oz dark/
bittersweet chocolate
1tbsp cocoa powder

AND

Freshly brewed coffee
Calvados (just bring the
bottle to the table)

Completely ready in advance, short of brewing a pot of coffee, this is a lovely dessert for the end of a dinner party. Your guests can eat it in whichever way they fancy – pouring the Calvados, or coffee, or both, over the ice-cream, or consuming them all separately. Vianne ends Armande's birthday meal with this; I can't think of anything lovelier or more wonderfully, warmly social.

Serves 8

1. Bring the cream and milk to simmering point over a low heat. Add the vanilla and the salt. Whisk the egg yolks and sugar until light and creamy. Whisking constantly, so as not to scramble the eggs, pour the hot cream and milk over them.

2. Wash out the pan and pour the custard back into it. Place over a low heat and cook, stirring constantly, until thick enough to coat the back of a wooden spoon. Remove from the heat, pour into a bowl, and leave to stand until room temperature.

3. Melt the chocolate in a heatproof bowl over a pan of gently simmering water. Remove from the heat and stir in the cocoa, then whisk this into the cooled custard. Cover with a plastic wrap, and refrigerate until chilled.

4. Transfer the ice cream to the freezer for 90 minutes, then whisk it vigorously to break up the ice crystals. Freeze for another hour, then whisk again, and repeat after another hour.

5. Remove the ice cream from the freezer 10 minutes before you're hoping to serve it. Put a generous scoop into a small bowl and serve alongside a little cup of coffee and a shot glass of Calvados, or bring the bottle and coffee pot to the table, and let people serve themselves.

From an English garden

First he ate some lettuces and some French beans; and then he ate some radishes.
The Tale of Peter Rabbit, Beatrix Potter

I spent long years dreaming of English gardens. Obsessed from an early age with *The Secret Garden* (and with Dickon, if I'm being entirely transparent), I longed to get dirt under my nails, and sit on a picnic blanket in an Edwardian dress and an enormous straw-brimmed hat. Aged eight, I arrived at my school's Book Day dressed in Mary's winter outfit: a wool skirt, hat, and gloves, with a wooden-handled skipping rope in my hands. It was March, and an unbearably warm day – my sullen face, as I realized my fatal error, was a perfect match for Mary Lennox's. And, like my fondness for wholly inappropriate outfits, my love of gardening was entirely vicarious; in real life, under the hot Australian sun, gardening was a sort of weekend punishment, something that had to be got through before I was allowed to pull my book out again.

When I arrived in England, I moved into a flat above a bank in Whitechapel. We had a concrete roof terrace, with a sofa my flatmate had found on the street, some temperamental pots of herbs, and a barbeque he made from an old oilcan. There was no getting away from the fact that it was mostly concrete. That spring, despite the rest of the city taking on a thousand shades of green, our street remained a persistent grey. I bought pots of lavender to keep above the sink in our kitchen, which helped, but I ached for a garden like the one Peter Rabbit raids, with rows of radishes, lettuces, and French beans to nibble on.

I now live in the countryside and, for the first time in my adult life, there are things growing in the garden that I can eat. Throughout spring I eat raw vegetables with gusto, as if I'd stumbled straight into Mr McGregor's garden. I dip peppery radishes, sweet asparagus, and Tenderstem broccoli into the rich yolks of boiled eggs. I eat slices of generously buttered bread, alongside a handful of peas to pod, or find baby lettuces to peel apart and eat leaf by leaf. Happy hours are spent finding infinite ways of bringing the abundance of spring into the kitchen.

Pork and broad bean burgers

50ml/3½tbsp Marsala
1tsp smoked paprika
1tsp fennel seeds
Salt and black pepper
400g/14oz minced/
ground pork

PURÉE

100g/¾ cup podded
broad/fava beans
75g/⅔ cup frozen peas,
defrosted
Zest and juice of 1 lemon
10 mint leaves
1tbsp olive oil
Salt and black pepper

AND

4 burger buns
A little butter and
mayonnaise

EQUIPMENT

Food processor

The first time I made a broad bean purée, I turned a Diana Henry recipe for six people into an accompaniment for a whole roasted pig at a wedding. It was very much my fault (she was clear it is a recipe for small groups), but I felt like I spent days of my life podding broad beans. It is to their eternal credit that it didn't put me off – not only are broad beans delicious, especially when fresh, but their soft, fuzzy beds are so satisfying to split open and run your thumb through.

Serves 4

1. Mix the Marsala, paprika, fennel seeds, and seasoning through the pork mince. Place into a covered bowl, or container, and transfer to the fridge for 24 hours so that the flavours have time to develop.

2. The next day, boil the broad beans for a minute, drain them, and pop their skins off.

3. In a food processor, blitz the cooled broad beans and peas with the zest and juice of the lemon, and the mint leaves. Add the olive oil and blitz again. Taste, and season with salt and pepper.

4. Shape the seasoned mince into 4 patties. Fry in a dry non-stick or cast-iron pan, for 8 minutes on each side. Turn the heat down if they're browning quickly; you want them to be cooked right through, but not burnt on the outside.

5. Toast the split buns in the still hot pan for a minute or two, and spread the top half with a little butter, and the bottom half with mayonnaise. Top with a generous spoonful of the purée and a patty. Serve immediately.

Asparagus and herb risotto

It's rare that I do anything to asparagus beyond balancing it over a pot of simmering water while I'm cooking a couple of eggs below. However, it is lovely in this risotto; thrown in at the last moment, so it still has a bite, and hasn't cooked down to mush.

Serves 2

1. Bring the stock to a simmer in a saucepan, and add the ends of the asparagus. Warm the butter and oil in a wide pan, and add the sliced shallots. Fry over a low heat for 5 minutes until softened.

2. Add the rice, and stir through the shallots for a couple of minutes. Pour over the vermouth, and allow it to bubble for a minute. Ladle a splash of the hot stock into the rice, and stir. Once the rice has soaked it up, add a splash more. Continue adding stock, stirring regularly (but not continuously – don't worry if you need to tackle a couple of other jobs while it's cooking) until the rice is close to cooked – it should still have a slight bite.

3. Slice the asparagus into 3cm/1¼in lengths. Fold through the rice. Add a little more stock, and stir for a final couple of minutes. Add the Parmesan, and turn off the heat.

4. Stir in the lemon zest, and the herbs. Taste and season. Spoon into bowls, top with fennel fronds (or dill, if you don't have any to hand), and squeeze some lemon juice over the top. Serve with more Parmesan.

1 litre/4¼ cups chicken or vegetable stock
150g/5½oz asparagus, woody ends snapped off for the stock
1tbsp butter
1tbsp olive oil
2 banana shallots, thinly sliced
150g/scant ¾ cup Arborio rice
100ml/scant ½ cup vermouth
60g/¾ cup grated Parmesan (or a vegetarian alternative)
Zest and juice of 1 lemon
Leaves from 6 sprigs thyme
20 mint leaves, chopped
Salt and black pepper
A few fennel or dill fronds, optional

Rhubarb and rose frozen yoghurt

800g/1¾lb rhubarb
150g/¾ cup golden
caster/superfine sugar
600ml/2¾ cups thick
natural yoghurt
1tbsp rosewater

I most associate rhubarb with the colder months – serving it on porridge or in crumbles, when it's cold and dark outside. But that's forced rhubarb, the tender type that's grown in the dark before the warmth of spring has time to work its magic on the tall, dark red stalks. This is a recipe for warm spring afternoons, and for late-season rhubarb, best eaten in the garden.

Serves at least 6

1. Preheat the oven to 180C fan/400F/gas 6. Slice the rhubarb into batons, and put in a single layer in a roasting dish. Sprinkle with a couple of tablespoons of the sugar, cover with foil, and bake for 20 minutes until soft. Leave to cool completely.

2. Whisk the yoghurt with the rest of the sugar, and the rosewater. Put in the freezer for an hour, whisk vigorously, and return to the freezer. Leave for another hour, then whisk again. Fold in the rhubarb, and return to the freezer for a couple of hours until solid.

3. Allow to soften for 5 minutes before serving.

Packing a picnic basket

It was hot enough now to make us seek the shade. On a sheep-cropped knoll under a clump of elms we ate the strawberries and drank the wine – as Sebastian promised, they were delicious together – and we lit fat, Turkish cigarettes and lay on our backs, Sebastian's eyes on the leaves above him, mine on his profile, while the blue-grey smoke rose, untroubled by any wind, to the blue-green shadows of foliage, and the sweet scent of the tobacco merged with the sweet summer scents around us…
Brideshead Revisited, Evelyn Waugh

A good picnic requires a perfect marriage of entirely uncontrollable elements. So often an afternoon on the grass, or the sand, is compromised by crowds of people who have had the same idea, by a family of wasps who want to make friends, by food spoiling, and drinks toppling over at the barest nudge. In my head I look like Brideshead's Lady Julia Flyte, all white linen and lace, cheeks flushed slightly in the heat. In reality, I'm a sweaty mess, out of practice with the sun and burning far too quickly as I desperately try to keep the food in the shade.

I have experimented with various picnic assemblages over the years; wrestled with sticky cakes that attract the ants, with yoghurt-based dips that barely make it to the park before they curdle, and with dressed salads that leak through ill-lidded Tupperware. But I have also had a fair few picnic successes: a day-long birthday feast featuring an enviable array of biscuits, sandwiches, quiches, and jugs of punch; salads and slices of cake enjoyed alongside a small pile of books on Hampstead Heath with my dad; and regular picnics on a blanket in London Fields, with boxes of food from Broadway Market, and bottles of ice-cold cider from the shop.

These successes are worth celebrating. When the uncontrollable elements come together, a picnic can feel like perfection. It's rare to happen across that dappled patch of shade, away from the crowds, on the gentlest of slopes so your glass doesn't wobble, with no wasps or ants to carry off your lunch, and (most importantly) with a basket of something delicious to hand, so you can take advantage of your good fortune. Embrace your inner Sebastian or Julia Flyte, lie back on the blanket, place an ostentatious hat over your eyes, and breathe in the early-summer air.

Curry puffs

1tbsp groundnut oil

2 banana shallots, finely diced

A 3cm/1¼in piece of ginger, peeled and grated

2 cloves garlic, minced

1tbsp hot curry powder

500g/1lb 2oz waxy potatoes, finely diced

400g/14oz minced/ ground chicken or turkey

1tsp light brown sugar

2tsp dark soy sauce

2tbsp mango chutney

500g/1lb 2oz puff pastry block, or 4 sheets of ready-rolled

1 egg

In Gerald Durrell's short story 'The Picnic', his mother's well-organized day out goes horribly wrong. Before it does, we hear of the spread she had planned, including (among other things) curry puffs, whole roast chickens, a treacle tart, homemade jams, meringues, and a fruitcake. It's worth noting that this is a picnic for six. Still, there's no faulting her taste; I love curry puffs. They're portable, like mini Cornish pasties, but lighter and easier to eat. They're good hot too, great to put in the middle of a table for a book club, or hand around with some bottles of beer while you watch a film.

Makes 16

1. Warm the oil in a frying pan and fry the shallots for 5 minutes, stirring so that they don't brown. Add the ginger and garlic and fry until fragrant. Stir in the curry powder, and cook for another couple of minutes.

2. Add the potatoes, and cook for 10 minutes, stirring regularly so that they don't stick. Add the mince, and stir it through. Once the meat is browned, add the sugar, soy sauce, and mango chutney, and cook for a final couple of minutes. Leave to cool.

3. Preheat the oven to 180C fan/400F/gas 6. Cut the pastry into quarters, and roll the first out to the thickness of a pound coin. Cut out discs, about 10cm/4in wide (use a small bowl as a guide). Beat the egg in a bowl, and use a pastry brush to paint a line around the edge of the circle. Spoon a couple of tablespoons of the meat mixture into the centre of the pastry, and then fold the circle over and press closed to seal. Paint the top with egg wash and use the back of a knife to make indents in the sealed edge, or crimp with a fork. Repeat with the rest of the pastry and filling.

4. Put the pastries on baking sheets lined with parchment paper, and transfer to the oven for 25 minutes, until risen, puffed, and golden. Serve with more mango chutney and yoghurt for dipping.

Cucumber sandwiches

There's nothing that makes me feel quite as fancy as cucumber sandwiches on a picnic. They're one of Charles Ryder's first images of Oxford – the women arriving and 'sight-seeing and pleasure-seeking, drinking claret cup, eating cucumber sandwiches; pushed in punts about the river'. What a glorious thing on a warm English day. The key here is some vinegar, and plenty of white pepper – cucumber sandwiches are hopelessly dull if they're underseasoned.

Makes 8 sandwiches, or 24 fingers

1. Slice the cucumbers into thin rounds and spread out on a plate. Sprinkle with a little salt and leave for 10 minutes so that some of the water leaches out. Pat down with a paper towel. Sprinkle the vinegar over the slices, and season with white pepper. Leave to sit for a couple of minutes.

2. To fill the sandwiches, spread cream cheese thickly on one slice of bread, and a scrape of butter on the other. Add a generous layer of cucumber, then a sprinkling of cress and chives. Close the sandwich, slice the top and bottom crusts off (retaining the side ones for stability) and slice into 3 fingers. Keep as cool as possible until you eat them.

2 cucumbers
½tsp salt
1tbsp white wine vinegar
White pepper
16 slices white bread (a sliced sandwich loaf is ideal)
150g/⅔ cup cream cheese
2tbsp butter
30g/1 cup cress
10g/¼ cup finely chopped chives

Spring in abundance

Brown butter and strawberry friands

125g/½ cup butter
4 egg whites
85g/scant 1 cup ground almonds
180g/1¼ cups icing/confectioner's sugar
50g/heaped ⅓ cup plain/all-purpose flour
½tsp ground ginger
A handful of strawberries, hulled and quartered

EQUIPMENT
Friand or muffin tray

These are lovely for a picnic: easy to make, a great vehicle for the first of the season's berries, and tolerant to being jostled around in a backpack as you head to the park. Play around with the spice, and the fruit, depending on your preference – these will be good with whatever soft fruit is available.

Makes 10–20, depending on the size of your tin

1. Preheat the oven to 180C fan/400F/gas 6. Melt the butter in a pan, swirling it over the heat until it browns and smells nutty. Tip into a bowl, to prevent it burning in the residual heat of the pan, and leave it to cool.*

2. Beat the egg whites until light and foamy, but not stiff, and then mix in the grounds almonds, sugar, flour, and ginger. Finally, fold in the browned butter. The mixture will be runny, but quite sticky.

3. Distribute between greased muffin moulds (or friand moulds, if you have them). The batter should make 6–12, depending on the size of your tin.

4. Drop some strawberry quarters into each friand. Bake large ones for 20 minutes, and small ones for 12. When done, they should be golden brown on top, and set in the middle; a skewer poked in should come out clean.

5. Allow to cool, then dust with icing sugar.

* Regular melted butter is absolutely fine here, but I love it like this. My friend Liv once gave me some brown butter friands, and now I can't make them without it.

Lemon verbena lemonade

On a hot summer's day in 1900, Mrs Appleyard's students piled into a trap and journeyed to Hanging Rock for a picnic. There is a strange atmosphere on the day; their watches stop at midday, they fall asleep in the long brown grass, and when they return to school, hours late, three students and a teacher have gone missing. But before all of that, when they're just a group a schoolgirls heading out on a picnic, there is lemonade in a zinc-lined basket that sits between them in the pony trap.

Serves at least 8

1. Put the lemon zest, juice, herbs, and sugar into a saucepan. Bring to a slow simmer and reduce until thickened and slightly viscous.

2. Cool in the pan, then strain into a bottle. Dilute 1 part syrup to 5 parts fizzy water to make the lemonade. Serve with extra lemon verbena leaves and plenty of ice.

LEMONADE
Zest and juice of 5 lemons
12 lemon verbena leaves
1 sprig rosemary
150g/¾ cup caster/superfine sugar

TO SERVE
1 bottle sparkling water
Lemon verbena leaves
Ice cubes

Sparkling jelly

150g/¾ cup caster/
superfine sugar
200ml/generous ¾ cup
water
9 sheets gelatin (or
enough for 900ml/
4 cups liquid)
750ml/3 cups sparkling
rosé
200g/1½ cups berries
(hulled strawberries
are lovely here, as are
raspberries)

EQUIPMENT LIST
Large serving bowl, or 6
fancy glasses

As Sebastian promised as he collected ingredients for a picnic at Brideshead, wine and berries make a delightful combination. A chilled bottle of fizz, and a box of berries, would be welcome in a picnic basket, but this jelly is also a complete joy. It's a simple dessert, but will hold up on a trip outdoors, so long as you don't leave it waiting in the sun for too long. You can serve these in cocktail or wine glasses instead of one big bowl – they'll just be a little less easy to transport.

Serves 6

1. Put the caster sugar and water in a saucepan, and simmer until syrupy. Meanwhile, put the gelatin sheets in a bowl of cold water, and leave for a couple of minutes to soak. Give them a squeeze, then stir into the hot syrup until dissolved. Pour into a large serving dish, or divide between individual glasses if that is how you're serving it.

2. Leave to cool for an hour out of the fridge, and then very slowly pour in the rosé – you want it to fizz as little as possible. Stir gently, and then cover and chill in the fridge for another hour.

3. Wash the berries, discarding any that are bruised. Drop them into the setting jelly and fold through until evenly dispersed. The jelly should fizz up a little. Set for at least 3 hours in the fridge, and keep cool until serving. It's great either plain or with some whipped cream.

Paris in springtime

*Very hungry, accustomed to English post-war food, Grace thought
the meal which followed the most delicious she had ever eaten. The
food, the wine, the heat, and the babel of French talk, most of which
was quite incomprehensible to her untuned ear, induced a half-drunk,
entirely happy state of haziness.*
The Blessing, Nancy Mitford

I had been in England only a couple of months when my flatmates
and I decided to go to Paris for the weekend. I had been before, but
in the company of grown-ups, and so this trip felt like the first time.
We booked tickets on the overnight coach, dozing on and off as
we travelled underneath the Channel, and arrived in the western
suburbs of the city just as the sun was coming up. We spent the
next couple of days wandering up and down the Seine, exploring
museums and parks and bars. We jumped on the train and visited
the gardens at Versailles, an almost lurid shade of green in the
rainy spring afternoon.

Paris had a lot to live up to. In my head, it was a city of mythic
proportions; the place that could transform Sabrina thanks to an
enviable haircut and a newly developed sense of independence,
that could provide a home and a refuge (in a very fancy apartment)
for Linda in *The Pursuit of Love*, that made Julia Child fall in love
with food, that saw Céline and Jesse knit their lives back together
in *Before Sunset*, that twinkled and glistened so invitingly in the
drawings in *Madeline*. I couldn't believe how easily it lived up to
expectation; how immediately I fell in love with it.

When I travel there now, I'm not leaving behind the post-war
English food the Mitfords complained about. But I do still always
look forward to eating in Paris: the early-morning pastries, eaten
hot from paper bags; oysters from the markets, served on a half
shell; the olives and crisps that come alongside a glass of wine;
delicious butter, spread thickly onto a fresh baguette. When I'm in
Paris, I eat out as much as possible – there are always far too many
things to try – but back home in England I cook like a Parisian,
leaving the croissants and fine patisserie to the professionals and
making only the simplest of dishes: meltingly soft omelettes,
toasted cheese sandwiches, and classic, simple salads.

Omelette aux fines herbes

This is a gloriously simple Sunday night supper, and also the sort of thing you could make in a tiny kitchen while on holiday – so long as you have a good non-stick pan, you need little else. This goes from ingredient to plate in a matter of seconds, so make sure you already have a glass of wine poured before you start cooking.

3 medium eggs
1tbsp single/light cream
Salt and black pepper
½tsp chopped chives
½tsp chopped tarragon
½tsp chopped chervil
½tsp chopped parsley
1tbsp unsalted butter

EQUIPMENT
Omelette pan or non-stick frying pan/skillet

Serves 1

1. Crack the eggs into a bowl and give them a really good whisk with a fork, until there are no remaining streaks of yolk or white. Add the cream and whisk again. Season with salt and pepper.

2. Place your chopped herbs, your bowl of egg, your fork (or spatula) and your serving plate close to the hob. This will all be over in a matter of seconds, and you don't want to be dashing around trying to find anything.

3. Place your pan over a high heat, and add the butter. Swirl the butter around so that the pan is well greased, but don't let it brown. Tip the eggs in and leave for a couple of seconds, then start moving the pan around vigorously, as you stir the eggs with your fork. Keep everything moving, until the bottom layer starts to look set, but the top is still liquid. Sprinkle the herbs over the top.

4. Tip your pan at a 45-degree angle, allowing most of the (still runny) omelette to slip down to one edge. Fold the top half over the bulk of the omelette. Turn off the heat.

5. Grasp your pan handle in your dominant hand, with your thumb on top and palm below. Hold your plate in the other hand, almost vertically, then bring the pan up to meet it. Tip the omelette onto the plate – the set underside will become the top. Eat immediately, while it's still warm and at the point of runny inside.

Salade Niçoise

SALAD
100g/3½oz new
potatoes
3 eggs
100g/¾ cup French
beans
150g/5½oz ripe
tomatoes
½ cucumber, deseeded
One Little Gem/Bibb
lettuce
50g/½ cup black olives,
pitted
2tbsp capers
6 anchovy fillets

DRESSING
2 cloves garlic, finely
chopped
2 anchovy fillets, finely
chopped
1tbsp red wine vinegar
1tsp Dijon mustard
3tbsp olive oil
Black pepper

Late in my teens, I travelled to France with a friend and
her mum. We spent a week bustling about a freezing Paris,
and then slowly travelled down the length of the country,
ending up in Nice. After a couple of weeks of frost and ice,
our days on the south coast felt like an entirely different
world. We ordered salade niçoise, surprised that it arrived
with plenty of sharp, salty anchovies, but without the tuna
I had come to expect. It was still the middle of winter, but
in Nice, in our t-shirts and jeans, eating at a table outside,
it felt like the height of spring.

Serves 2

1. Bring the new potatoes to the boil in a saucepan of salted
water, and cook for 10 minutes until tender. Bring a second
saucepan to the boil and add the eggs. Boil for 7 minutes,
then run under cold water, and set aside. Cook the beans in
boiling water for 3 minutes and then blanch in cold water.

2. Cut a cross in the base of each tomato, and cover with
boiling water. Leave for a minute, then remove and plunge
into ice-cold water. Peel off the skins, slice into chunks and
remove the seeds. Slice the cucumber and lettuce. Toss the
potatoes, beans, tomatoes, cucumber, lettuce, olives, and
capers together in a bowl.

3. Put the dressing ingredients in a jar, and shake vigorously
to emulsify. Pour over the salad, and toss together. Divide
between 2 plates. Peel the eggs, and slice into wedges. Top
each salad with wedges of egg, and whole anchovy fillets.

Croque Monsieur

The image of *The Dud Avocado*'s Sally Jay Gorce, hungry late at night, and making a trip down to her local café for a croque monsieur and a hot chocolate, is a model for us all. Inspired by her, this has become my 2 a.m. specialty – the kind of thing I end up making after a night out with pals, or when I'm up late writing. It's even more comforting than a classic cheese toastie (if such a thing were possible), and benefits from as much mustard as you can handle, to cut through the rich cheese sauce.

Serves 2

1. Turn on your grill/broiler. Put the 4 slices of bread on a rack, and toast on one side until just golden – keep an eye on them or they'll burn.

2. Make the cheese sauce. Melt the butter in a small saucepan, and then add the flour. Cook for a couple of minutes. Add the milk, a splash at a time, along with the bay leaf. Cook, stirring, until thickened, then add the cheese. Season with white pepper and nutmeg, and set aside.

3. Place one slice of bread, toasted-side down, back on the grill rack. Spread with butter, and then generously with mustard. Top with ham and then cheese, and pop back under the grill for a minute, until the cheese is starting to melt. Top with a second slice of toast, toasted-side up, and spoon over the warm cheese sauce (leaving the bay leaf behind in the pan).

4. Place back under the grill, and cook until the cheese sauce is bubbling and golden brown. Serve immediately.

SAUCE
1tbsp butter
1tbsp flour
150ml/⅔ cup milk
1 bay leaf
50g/½ cup grated Gruyère
White pepper
A pinch of grated nutmeg

SANDWICHES
4 slices bread
1tbsp butter
A generous spread of Dijon mustard
100g/¾ cup thinly sliced ham
50g/½ cup grated Gruyère

And a few more books for you to turn to when the garden is lush and green...

Choose bread and butter over cake (the latter is rarely seen in the best houses these days), and consider *The Importance of Being Earnest*. Explore Prince Edward Island, and make a batch of raspberry cordial for Diana, with *Anne of Green Gables*. Join the rabbits in *Watership Down* as the primroses are ending, and the May sunset is red in the clouds. Paddle on the edge of the seashore with the family in *The Big Alfie and Annie Rose Storybook*. Travel to California with the Winter family to escape the cold, and spend time on set with Jane in *The Painted Garden*. Pack a pot of hunny, and have a stroll through the Hundred Acre Wood with *Winnie-the-Pooh*, Piglet, and Christopher Robin, of course. Sneak off to the cottage for the afternoon with *Lady Chatterley's Lover*. Enjoy the spring, and the slightly warmer water, at *The Lido* with Rosemary and Kate. Spend a very different (impossibly bleak) Easter on *The Loney* with Harry and his brother. Ensure that you give some time, on Bloomsday, to discovering Dublin with *Ulysses*'s Leopold Bloom.

The height
of summer

The height of summer

Summer afternoon—summer afternoon; to me those have always been the two most beautiful words in the English language.
Henry James

As a child, I spent most of the hot summer days sitting out of the sun, with a book in my hands. Summers are busy now, but for the first two decades of my life, I had the seemingly endless school and university holidays, with little to do but lie in a hammock, or on the beach, and swap books back and forth with my sister. In the summer months, we visited Maycomb County with Scout, Jem, and Dill, played about on boats with Arthur Ransome's Swallows and Amazons, wandered the Australian outback with the Magic Pudding and his comrades, and lay in the long Devonshire grass with Marianne and Elinor Dashwood. We read insatiably, revisiting our favourites over and over and bringing home piles from the library to stack up on our desks.

The summer heat in Queensland is almost unbearable. When we returned to school each January, we'd appear extraordinarily dedicated for the first weeks, lining up outside our classrooms long before lessons started. In reality, with only one ceiling fan in each room, our early arrival was a competition – as soon as a teacher unlocked the door, we'd elbow each other out of the way to fight for the position underneath it. When I left Australia, aged twenty-one, I was adamant I would never come back to visit in the summer, certain I had left that sort of weather behind for good. Inevitably, whoever is in charge of the changing seasons seems to have had a different idea. I'm writing these words in the midst of the type of summer I thought I'd never see again, this time in the English countryside. A hosepipe ban is imminent, the hills and fields outside the window are a dry, crisp yellow, and the heat sits heavily over us. We're not equipped for it: not our dispositions, nor our houses, nor our transport system (a summer journey on London Underground's Central Line is a special kind of hell).

For the most part, it's reminded me that summer still isn't my season – the heat makes it impossible for me to get involved in much beyond sitting quietly in the corner. I am loath to spend hours in a kitchen with the oven on, or stand at the hob for more than a few

minutes. I bake once the sun has gone down, or not at all. But this year, for the first time, I am appreciating the quiet joys of summer. The long, calm evenings, the late-afternoon sun striking my shoulders, the impromptu barbeques that happen in gardens along our street. And each Saturday, at the market, I have fallen upon a glut of some fruit or vegetable, greeting it as I would a friend who has returned, long anticipated, from time away. Regardless of whether I fancy cooking, my kitchen is always full – of tomatoes, of stone fruit, of vibrant beautiful berries. I stock the fridge with fresh fish, employ herbs in generous handfuls, and always have at least one dessert in the freezer. I may not love the heat, but the ingredients it offers up mean that I am rarely happier with the food on my plate than I am in the summer.

The heady scent of tomatoes

Tomato Day. Oh God, if anyone found out about it I'd die. There we sat, last Saturday, in my grandmother's backyard, cutting the bad bits off over-ripe tomatoes and squeezing them. After doing ten crates of those, we boiled them, squashed them, then boiled them again. That in turn made spaghetti sauce. We bottled it in beer bottles and stored it in Nonna's cellar.
Looking for Alibrandi, Melina Marchetta

We used to grow tomatoes in the corner of our garden. When it was my turn to water them before school, I would point the hose in their general direction, and sit with a book, waiting for the allotted time to pass so I could head back inside for breakfast. Underneath their fuzzy leaves, the tomatoes would turn from green to orange to red, swelling as they darkened, and giving off a heady scent I still associate with those unbearably hot Brisbane summers.

I might have been ambivalent towards my job of watering the plants, but I have never been anything but enthusiastically dedicated to the fruit itself. As a teen, I would have happily subsisted on tricolore salad alone. I eat tomatoes like apples, biting straight through the firm, fragrant skin, and allowing their seeds to drip through my fingers. A bowl of cherry tomatoes left on the kitchen countertop will disappear slowly but steadily over the course of a day as I pass back and forth.

When I squash a deep-red tomato in my palm, or simmer a batch of them on the stove, I think of Melina Marchetta's *Looking for Alibrandi*. I think of Josie Alibrandi's exasperation with her sprawling extended family, about the fact that they are all entirely and unapologetically themselves, and about their infamous tomato day. If you, like the Alibrandis (or my family, when our plants were generous with their fruit), are lucky enough to bring home a glut of tomatoes, I have a few recipe suggestions over the following pages. You can, of course, bottle the whole lot to last you through the cold winter (p. 158). But I've always been just as happy to use tins out of season, so I can commit myself to eating whatever I can get my hands on through the glorious summer months.

Basic tomato pasta sauce

1.5kg/3lb 5oz very ripe tomatoes (these need to be full of flavour and to smell of summer)
Salt and black pepper
1tbsp caster/superfine sugar
2tbsp red wine vinegar

If you have a few bottles of this stored in your kitchen, you are never more than ten minutes from dinner. It's a wonderful way to capture the height of tomato season – kept in sealed bottles, this will give you a taste of summer all year round. Channel the Alibrandis here if you can – start with as many tomatoes as possible, and sit around in the back garden, the sun on your shoulders, hands covered in tomato seeds, surrounded by bowls full of pulped flesh.

Makes enough to fill at least a couple of large bottles/jars*
1. Pull the tomatoes off their vines, cut out the core and make a cross with your knife where you have removed it. Blanch in a pan of boiling water for 1 minute, then remove with a slotted spoon and place straight into iced water. The skins will now slip off easily. Do this in batches, or the tomatoes will cool the boiling water down when you drop them all in.

2. Squash the tomatoes to a pulp with your hands (take time over this bit and really enjoy it). Place over a low to medium heat to bubble away for about an hour. Push the sauce through a sieve to remove the seeds and boil again for another 20 minutes. You should have a rich, thick sauce.

3. Season with salt, pepper, sugar, and vinegar. Pour into hot, sterilized bottles for storage.

* Sterilize your bottles by washing them out, putting them in the sink, and pouring boiling water into them until it flows over the top. Once they're cool enough to touch, tip the water out, and dry them completely in a very low oven (be sure to remove any plastic fittings or seals before you put them into the oven). Fill them while warm.

Polenta and roasted tomatoes

This is a tomato dish for a cooler evening – after a late-afternoon downpour, perhaps. It's comforting, but still bright and sharp: a bowl of soft polenta, rich with goat's cheese, topped with roasted tomatoes and drizzled with balsamic. It takes full advantage of the tomato season, but is still appropriate for those inevitable English summer nights that make you want to pull a cardigan out of storage.

Serves 2, very generously

1. The evening before you want to eat this, preheat the oven to 180C fan/400F/gas 6. Slice the tomatoes in half and place them cut-side up in a roasting tray lined with parchment paper. Drizzle with the olive oil, and season. Roast for 45 minutes, until caramelized around the edges. Leave the oven door ajar and let the tomatoes cool in there overnight, or for at least an hour. Store in an airtight container.*

2. To make the polenta, bring the stock and milk to a simmer in a saucepan. Pour the polenta into the pan in a thin stream, whisking constantly. Whisk over a low-medium heat for 5 minutes, until thick.

3. Whisk in the butter and cheese, then taste and season. Spoon into bowls and serve with the roasted tomatoes, fresh thyme leaves, and a drizzle of balsamic vinegar.

* Extra tomatoes (and there will be plenty) are great on toast for breakfast, or in the panzanella overleaf.

ROASTED TOMATOES
1kg/2lb 4oz fresh tomatoes (plum tomatoes are great here)
50ml/3½tbsp olive oil
Salt and black pepper

POLENTA
350ml/1½ cups chicken stock
250ml/1 cup milk
175g/scant 1¼ cups quick-cook polenta
30g/2tbsp butter
70g/scant 1 cup hard goat's cheese, grated
A pinch of salt

TO SERVE
Leaves from 3 sprigs of thyme
Balsamic vinegar

Panzanella

This is my favourite salad: summery, vibrant, full of flavour, and a breeze to put together. It's a fantastic showcase for tomatoes, utilizing meltingly soft ones that have collapsed in the oven, as well as fragrant, fresh, firm-skinned ones. If you find some gorgeous green ones, slice them and add them in too (it's a more summer-appropriate use for them than heating a pan of oil for the fried green tomatoes in Idgie's Whistle Stop Café). The proportions below are a guide – if you love capers, add more; if you're not a fan of roasted pepper, leave it out. Salads are incredibly forgiving.

Serves 4

1 red/bell pepper
1 red onion
2tbsp red wine vinegar
4 thick slices of day-old ciabatta
4 ripe tomatoes, sliced
A large handful of cherry tomatoes
12 roasted tomato halves (see p. 159)
A handful of basil leaves
2 balls mozzarella, torn into chunks
3tbsp capers
50ml/3½tbsp olive oil
Salt and black pepper

1. Preheat the oven to 220C fan/475F/gas 9. Rub a large red pepper with a little olive oil, and roast, turning a couple of times, until black all over. It should take 25 minutes or so. If you have a barbeque, or a gas hob, you can do this over the flame, if you'd prefer. Allow it to cool in a plastic bag, then peel off the charred skin, pull out the seeds, and cut into strips.

2. Thinly slice the red onion and soften in the red wine vinegar while you prepare the rest of the salad.

3. Tear the bread into chunks. Toss together with the fresh tomatoes, roasted pepper, roasted tomatoes, basil, mozzarella, the capers and the onion.

4. Make a dressing with the vinegar from the onion, the olive oil, a teaspoon of caper juice, salt and plenty of pepper. Whisk together until emulsified.

5. Dress the salad at least 20 minutes before you want to serve it, so the bread has time to soften a little in the dressing.

A midsummer party

They set the table for four. There would be the herring and pork and
potatoes, and two kinds of vegetables. And marinated pears for dessert.
'He doesn't eat dessert,' said Sophia nervously. 'And he doesn't eat
vegetables either. He calls it grass. You know that.'
'Yes, I know,' Grandmother said. 'But it looks nice.'
The Summer Book, Tove Jansson (translated by Thomas Teal)

We don't celebrate midsummer in Australia – it falls mere days
before Christmas, so has long been overshadowed by tinsel,
turkey, and paper hats – but since moving to the UK, and spending
midsummer with my half-Swedish family, it's become one of my
favourite culinary holidays. From my first summer here, I fell in
love with it: a midsummer pole in the garden, a rich cheese tart in
the oven, floral garlands in our hair, and bottles of freshly made
elderflower cordial on the table.

In Queensland, summer days are not that much longer than
winter ones, and so my early experiences of the changing seasons
were very much to do with temperature, rather than light. But in
Northern Europe, the longest day of the year is something that
deserves to be marked. It's not only the most light we'll see all year,
but a quiet reminder that the days will now start to get shorter as
we head towards autumn, and then winter.

This is even more tangible in Scandinavia, where the endless
nights of winter mean there may be less than an hour of light each
day, a contrast to their summer days, when the sun never quite
vanishes beneath the horizon. It's why the days in Tove Jansson's
The Summer Book feel bright, and endless, and full of possibility –
because, quite literally, they are. Even in England, when the sun
sets around 10 p.m., scenes of midsummer parties feel magical:
the long lunch and dancing in Sarah Perry's *The Essex Serpent* or
the glorious wedding in *Cold Comfort Farm*. It's also the day that
The Amber Spyglass's Lyra and Will promise to spend on a bench
in Oxford each year, remembering their time together. In short,
midsummer is a day worth celebrating. In our house, that means a
smörgåsbord spread, served late in the afternoon, which covers the
whole table. Nothing hot from the oven, just crisp salads, herring,
and my favourite: that famous cheese tart.

Västerbottenostpaj (Swedish cheese tart)

This is a gorgeous centerpiece for the midsummer table: a salty, rich tart that works best alongside salads full of still-tender vegetables, pickles, and leafy greens dressed with a sharp vinaigrette. It's better the day after you bake it too, so do what I do, and put it in the oven once the sun goes down the day before midsummer.

Serves 12 as part of a smörgåsbord

1. In a food processor, blitz the flour and butter until they resemble breadcrumbs. You can do this with your hands, by rubbing the butter into the flour using only your fingertips, but the pastry is quite buttery, and can be difficult to work with in summer. Add the water, a little at a time, until the pastry comes together in a ball.

2. Wrap the pastry in plastic wrap, and refrigerate for at least half an hour.

3. Preheat the oven to 200C fan/425F/gas 7. Roll out the pastry to the thickness of a coin, and use it to line a tart tin. Patch up any tears in the pastry, and prick the base all over with a fork. Return to the fridge for half an hour.

4. Line the pastry with a couple of sheets of plastic wrap, and then fill with baking beans or rice. Bake for 20 minutes, then remove the plastic wrap and beans, and bake for a further 10 minutes, until a deep golden brown.

5. Meanwhile, make the filling. Beat the eggs, cream, and milk together, and season with the cayenne and white pepper. Add the grated cheese. The cheese is very salty, so you shouldn't need to add salt.

6. Reduce the oven temperature to 180C fan/400F/gas 6, pour the filling into the tart case, and bake for 30 minutes, until browned on top. The filling will puff up, but will fall again once it's out of the oven. Serve at room temperature, cut into slices.

PASTRY
300g/2¼ cups plain/all-purpose flour
180g/¾ cup cold butter
2tbsp cold water

FILLING
4 eggs
350ml/1½ cups double/heavy cream
150ml/⅔ cup milk
1tsp cayenne pepper
A generous pinch of white pepper
300g/10oz Västerbottenost,* grated

EQUIPMENT
Large loose-bottomed tart tin/pan (I use a 25 x 20cm/10 x 8in rectangular one, but a deep round one would work too).

*You can find it in IKEA (of course) or online, or you can substitute a mix of mature Cheddar and Gruyère.

Herring, mustard, rye crispbread

RYE CRISPBREAD

300g/2 cups rye flour

4g/1tsp easy-action yeast

1tsp salt

250ml/1 cup warm water

1tsp caraway seeds

1tsp fennel seeds

1tsp nigella seeds

1tsp sesame seeds

HERRING WITH MUSTARD

500g/1lb 2oz salted herring fillets, rinsed, soaked in fresh water overnight, and drained

2 egg yolks

1tbsp cider vinegar

200ml/generous ¾ cup groundnut oil

1tbsp Dijon mustard

1tbsp grainy mustard (ideally Swedish)

¼tsp sugar

A handful of dill fronds

Every Christmas we eat tiny boiled potatoes alongside various types of pickled herring, which we pick up at IKEA in the final months of the year. They come flavoured with dill, with carrots, onion and juniper, and (my favourite) with mustard dressing. Though it's lovely as a start to our Christmas Eve meal, I like it even better in summer, on homemade crispbread with really great butter.

Enough for a starter for 8

1. First, make the crispbread. Put the flour in a bowl, with the yeast on one side, and the salt on the other. Pour in the water, and mix with your hand. Knead for 5 minutes until a little less sticky (it will still be quite sticky, so keep your hands oiled), cover the bowl, and leave to rise for an hour.

2. Preheat the oven to 200C fan/425F/gas 7. Divide the dough into 18 equal pieces, and roll each into a ball. To flatten them out, rub olive oil into your hands so they don't stick, and press them out directly onto the parchment paper you will bake them on. Press until they are 2mm/ $\frac{1}{16}$in thick and prick all over with a fork. Mix the seeds together and sprinkle over the crispbreads.

3. Bake in the oven for 15–18 minutes, until crisp – you may need to do this in batches. Allow to cool completely and store in an airtight container – they'll stay crisp for 2–3 days if you want to make them in advance.

4. For the herring, rinse the salted fillets, and cut into thick slices. Put the egg yolks in a bowl with the cider vinegar, and whisk. Dribble in the groundnut oil, whisking constantly. Continue adding until the mixture thickens into a mayonnaise. Whisk in the mustards and sugar.

5. Stir the herring into the sauce, coating each piece completely, and then add the dill. Store in a container in the fridge; the herring will keep for a couple of days like this. Serve alongside the crispbread, and a dish of good butter.

Swedish eggs

No smörgåsbord would be complete without a plate of these. Half an egg each might suffice if you've got lots of other things on the table, but I'd err on the side of having plenty.

Enough for a starter for 8

1. Bring a pot of water to the boil. Lower the eggs in, gently, so they don't crack when they hit the bottom. Simmer for 7 minutes, then run them under cold water until cool enough to touch.

2. Crack the shells all over, peel the eggs, and slice them in half. Place cut-side up on a serving plate, and squeeze a swirl of caviar onto each egg. Top with a sprig of dill, and a tiny pinch of white pepper.

8 eggs, at room temperature
3tbsp Kalles Kaviar*
16 dill fronds
White pepper

* Kalles Kaviar, or creamed cod roe, can be found in luridly colourful tubes at Swedish food shops or IKEA. Once you have it in your fridge, squeeze it onto rye toast with boiled eggs for breakfast; it won't last long.

Something crisp and colourful

With the cheese tart, eggs, and a rich mustard sauce, I always appreciate something crisp and fresh to munch on too. If you can get your hands on bright, sweet vegetables, all they'll need is a tiny splash of a sharp dressing.

Enough for a starter for 8

1. Slice the carrots and asparagus lengthways. Slice the radishes thinly, using a mandoline if you have one. Put the vegetables into a bowl of ice-cold water, and leave them to crisp up for 5–10 minutes.

2. Drain the vegetables, and pat them dry. Whisk together the vinegar and the oil, and then toss the vegetables in the dressing. Arrange on a serving plate and dress with dill sprigs, and a generous grinding of pepper.

8 baby carrots
16 stems asparagus
8 radishes
2tsp white wine vinegar
2tsp cold-pressed rapeseed/canola oil
A handful of dill fronds
Black pepper

Swedish potato salad

2kg/4lb 8oz tiny new potatoes

250ml/generous 1 cup crème fraîche/sour cream

100g/scant ½ cup mayonnaise

2tbsp pickle juice, from the jar of cornichons

Salt and white pepper

50g/⅓ cup cornichons, chopped

3tbsp capers

6 dill fronds

Fennel fronds, if you have some

I adore potato salad. It's often the first thing I will go for in a big buffet or smörgåsbord. It's also the first recipe I remember learning from a novel. When I was ten, I was given a box set of Linda Bailey's Stevie Diamond mysteries. In the third book, *Who's Got Gertie? And How Can We Get Her Back!*, teenage sleuth Stevie prepares a potato salad for a pot luck and reveals her family's secret ingredient: a spoonful of pickle juice. I have included this in almost all my potato salads ever since.

Serves 8, or more on a smörgåsbord

1. Boil the potatoes in salted water until tender. Drain and leave to cool.

2. In the serving bowl, whisk together the crème fraîche, mayonnaise, pickle juice and seasoning.

3. Add the potatoes, cornichons, capers, and dill, and mix together. Top with fennel fronds if you have some, and serve.

Elderflower gelato and macerated strawberries

In Sarah Perry's *The Essex Serpent*, Cora hosts a midsummer party. After a meal of capons roasted with thyme, ham studded with cloves, salmon dressed with lemon, and a tomato salad with mint, she serves strawberries for dessert, dredged with sugar. It's one of the best possible summer desserts; English strawberries are, at their best (around midsummer), a dream. Only a scoop of ice cream alongside improves them.

Serves 8

1. Bring the milk and cream to a simmer in the saucepan. Put the cornflour in a bowl, and pour over a dribble of the milk mixture. Whisk with a fork to a smooth paste, then add to the milk in the pan. Whisk to incorporate. Add the salt. Stir over a low heat until thick enough to coat the back of a wooden spoon.

2. Take off the heat, and stir in the elderflower cordial. Cool completely in the fridge.

3. To freeze, either pour the chilled custard into an ice-cream maker, or into a container that can go into the freezer. Churn the custard until it looks like a soft-serve, or whisk every hour as it solidifies in the freezer. Once it reaches a soft-serve texture, add the lemon curd to the ice cream in big spoonfuls, and use a flat knife to ribbon it through. Freeze until solid.

4. Hull the strawberries and slice evenly. Sprinkle with the sugar, season with a little pepper, and toss with your hands. Bring the gelato out of the freezer 10 minutes before you want to serve; it will need a little time to soften. Serve in scoops with the strawberries.

GELATO
500ml/2 cups milk
250ml/1 cup double/heavy cream
4tsp cornflour/cornstarch
A pinch of salt
175ml/¾ cup elderflower cordial
150g/½ cup lemon curd*

AND
400g/4 cups strawberries
50g/heaped ⅓ cup icing/confectioner's sugar
Black pepper

* A jar of shop-bought lemon curd will work well here, though you may prefer making your own if you have some lemons in the fruit bowl. If you fancy it, omit the passionfruit pulp in the curd on p. 189 and replace it with extra lemon juice.

Marquees and wedding season

The table was laid under the cart-shed. On it were four sirloins, six chicken fricassees, stewed veal, three legs of mutton, and in the middle a fine roast suckling pig, flanked by four chitterlings with sorrel. At the corners were decanters of brandy. Sweet bottled-cider frothed round the corks, and all the glasses had been filled to the brim with wine beforehand.
Madame Bovary, Gustave Flaubert (translated by Eleanor Marx-Aveling)

It is possible that I will always associate summer days in England with weddings. In my late twenties, in addition to the inevitable period of life that brings successive wedding invitations, I began to cater them too. With my great friend and catering partner Liv, I have built kitchens in fields, garages, church halls, and gardens. But, as with so many firsts (a first snog at a year-nine dance, as 'Oh Mickey' played; my first night in England, jetlagged and emotional in a friend's spare room in Mile End), it is the first wedding that has remained memorable and distinct.

I made so many dreadfully naïve decisions, planning a near-impossible menu, assuming I knew how long it would take to peel twenty kilograms of potatoes, pod piles of broad beans, and fill hundreds of rice-paper rolls with julienned vegetables. The day itself was a comedy of errors: a team of wasp-stung kitchen staff, temperatures over thirty-five degrees in the catering tent and canisters of water that had to be refilled from a tap hundreds of metres away through animal paddocks and swinging gates. As the guests took to the dance floor, we collapsed in near-hysterical laughter.

Years on, it's the story we tell when we're all together. Because, alongside the anecdotes, we created a meal for over two hundred people that day, including a whole roasted pig. Serving it felt like the realization of the many dreams I had had about feasts in literature. There is something inescapably medieval about cooking a large animal whole; it is a feat so few of us will ever have cause to strive for. It puts me in mind of Henry VIII in *Wolf Hall*, of the roasted pig in Homer's *The Odyssey*, of Shakespeare's feasts, of Madame Bovary's extravagant wedding breakfast and of the enormous dining room in William Goldman's *The Princess Bride*.

Lemon and thyme cake

CAKE

400g/2 cups golden caster/superfine sugar

200g/¾ cup + 2tbsp unsalted butter

4 eggs

Zest of 3 lemons

440g/3⅓ cups plain/all-purpose flour

2½tsp baking powder

1tsp bicarbonate of soda/baking soda

A pinch of salt

200ml/generous ¾ cup milk

80ml/⅓ cup lemon juice

30g/1 cup chopped thyme leaves

ICING

140g/1 cup egg whites (about 9 eggs)

225g/heaped 1 cup golden caster/superfine sugar

½tsp salt

¼tsp cream of tartar

375g/1⅔ cups unsalted butter, softened

1tsp vanilla bean paste

DECORATION

Thyme sprigs

Edible flowers

EQUIPMENT

20cm/8in loose-bottomed cake tin/pan with tall sides (or 2 shallower ones)

Electric whisk or mixer

The tragedy of a wedding cake, so often only requested for the sake of the photographs, is that it ends up uneaten and unloved, drooping in the corner by the end of the day. It's a sad sight; I always picture Miss Havisham, sat beside her ancient, moulding cake. Make sure you pick a cake you love if you're planning a wedding, and do take every possible opportunity to make a fancy cake for a lower-key celebration too – this one is the perfect size for a birthday party (or can be doubled or tripled to make a wedding cake). It's a proper crowd pleaser. The icing here is Stella Parks' and is a great one to use for any event where the cake has to stand tall for a good couple of hours.

Cuts into 16 generous pieces

1. Preheat the oven to 160C fan/350F/gas 4. Grease and line the cake tin.

2. Cream together the sugar and butter until light and no longer grainy. Beat in the eggs, one at a time. Don't worry too much if it splits – it will come back together when you start adding the flour. Add the lemon zest.

3. In a separate bowl, sieve together the flour, baking powder, bicarbonate of soda, and salt. Add this to the creamed butter and sugar, a spoonful at a time, alternating with splashes of the milk. Continue until both are used up.

4. Fold in the lemon juice and the thyme leaves.

5. Bake for 50 minutes to 1 hour. The cake should be golden brown and well risen, and a skewer inserted into the middle of the cake should come out clean.

6. Cool the cake for 10 minutes in its tin, and then completely on a wire rack.

7. To make the icing, put the egg whites, sugar, salt, and cream of tartar in a large heatproof bowl, and place over a pan of simmering water. Stir constantly with a spoon or spatula, until the mixture reaches 85C/185F. Take off the

heat, and beat with an electric whisk on a medium speed to stiff peaks. Keep beating until it cools; this will take about 5 minutes.

8. Start adding the butter, a tablespoon at a time, while beating on a medium speed. The icing will deflate and might be too liquid at some points, but have faith – it will thicken again. Once thick and holding stiff peaks, beat in the vanilla paste.

9. Slice the cake in half, or in thirds, depending on how much icing you want in it. Place the bottom layer of the cake on a serving plate. Spread with a generous layer of icing, and add the other layer/s. Once the cake is assembled, with icing between the layers, apply a 'crumb coat': a thin layer of icing to keep crumbs out of the outer layer of icing. Place in the fridge for an hour to firm up again.

10. Spread a thicker layer of icing over the cake, and smooth out with a dough scraper, spatula, or flat knife. Place back in the fridge to firm up. Decorate with fresh thyme and edible flowers.*

* Before you rush out into the garden to collect blooms for your cake, a couple of tips:
» A number of aesthetically pleasing flowers are poisonous, so shouldn't end up anywhere near your cake. Only use flowers you're confident of – nasturtiums, cornflowers, and violas are a safe start.
» Flowers from a florist are often sprayed with chemicals, so use specific edible flower suppliers (like Maddocks Farm Organics in the UK) instead.
» Flowers wilt if left for too long. Store them in the fridge, and decorate at the last minute.

Broccoli, red onion, lemon, and caper salad

When we talk to people about catering their weddings, the conversation often starts with meat: whether they want whole chickens, rubbed with butter and thyme and roasted until golden, shoulders of lamb seasoned with spicy harissa, or a joint of pork with crisp crackling. Personally, though, I am always more interested in the salads. Vibrant and full of flavour, they are what make the table special, and what people go away remembering. This is one of my favourites: easy to make in large quantities, and a happy companion for whatever else you have on the table.

Serves 6 (though very easy to scale up)

1. Preheat the oven to 180C fan/400F/gas 6. Slice the broccoli tops into large florets, and set aside the stems for the pesto. Put the florets into a roasting tray, drizzle with 3 tablespoons of the olive oil and season generously. Roast until crisp and brown in places; about 40 minutes.

2. Cover the sliced onion with the juice of the lemon, squeeze with your fingers to soften it, and set aside. Toast the flaked almonds in a dry pan until golden, remove from the pan, and then toast the whole almonds (for the pesto) for a minute or so.

3. Make the broccoli pesto. Chop the broccoli stems into chunks and put into a food processor. Blitz until the broccoli is finely chopped, and then add the whole almonds and cheese. Blitz again, and season with salt and pepper. While the food processor runs, pour in the olive oil in a steady stream until you have a thick sauce.

4. To serve, place the roasted broccoli florets on a platter, and toss them with the leaves from the bunch of parsley. Put the softened onion over the top, and add spoonfuls of the pesto. Warm the final tablespoon of oil in the pan, and fry the capers until crisp. Pour the capers and oil over the salad. Top with the flaked almonds, and serve.

SALAD
3 heads broccoli
4tbsp olive oil
Salt and black pepper
1 red onion, sliced
Juice of 1 lemon
40g/ ½ cup flaked/ slivered almonds
A large bunch of parsley
2tbsp capers

BROCCOLI PESTO
40g/⅓ cup whole almonds
30g/⅓ cup grated hard goat's cheese
Salt and black pepper
Up to 100ml/scant ½ cup olive oil

EQUIPMENT
Food processor

Pork belly and roasted fennel

1.5kg/3lb 5oz pork belly
1tbsp fennel seeds
1tbsp flaky sea salt
1tsp black peppercorns
2 brown onions, roughly chopped
2 stalks celery, roughly chopped
2 medium carrots, roughly chopped
5 bay leaves
10 sprigs thyme
3 small bulbs fennel
200ml/generous ¾ cup vermouth
24 gooseberries
2tbsp plain/all-purpose flour
500ml/2 cups chicken stock
1tsp Dijon mustard

At the first wedding we catered, I roasted a whole pig. If you ever find yourself in the same situation, treat it simply: make deep cuts in the skin and rub coarse salt and fennel seeds over the whole thing, then roast it over a fire, or in a specially designed oven. For a more reasonably sized event, a cut of pork belly is entirely sufficient. It's also a joy in summer: leave it in a low oven, and eat it warm, rather than hot, with some seasonal fennel and sharp fruit.

Serves 6

1. Preheat the oven to 220C fan/475F/gas 9. Score the skin of the pork, cutting through the fat, but not the meat. Grind the fennel seeds, salt, and pepper together in a mortar and pestle, then rub the spices into the skin of the pork.

2. Arrange the chopped vegetables in one layer in the bottom of a roasting tin. Add the bay leaves and thyme. Place the pork on top and transfer to the oven.

3. Leave for 15 minutes in the blisteringly hot oven, before reducing it to 150C fan/340F/gas 3. Roast for 2 hours.

4. Slice the fennel bulbs in half lengthways. Pull the tray out of the oven, tip in the vermouth and 500ml/2 cups water, and nestle the fennel in among the vegetables. Return to the oven for an hour and a half. In the final 15 minutes, add the gooseberries to the pan.

5. Test the meat with a fork – you want it to be falling apart. Pull it out of the pan, and leave it to rest under a loose tent of foil. Remove the gooseberries and fennel, and set aside.

6. Place the contents of the tray, including the soft vegetables, over a low heat. Add the flour, and stir it through the vegetables and meat juices. Cook for a couple of minutes. Add the chicken stock and stir until thickened. Finally, taste and season with salt, pepper, and the mustard. Strain, and serve with the meat, gooseberries, and fennel.

Sixteen (chicken) oyster pie

Leftovers are the best part of wedding catering. One time, as I carved eight large chickens, I put the backs – the oysters, and the scraps – in a little box to take home and turn into a pie the next day. I admit: this recipe is not at all summery. But sometimes, in the midst of the warmest months, when I'm exhausted, or poorly, I want to draw the curtains, turn on a fan, bake a pie, and pretend it's winter.

Serves 4, or just a couple of you with leftovers

1. First, make the pastry. Rub the cold butter into the flour, and bring together with an egg yolk. Try to work it as little as possible, then wrap and chill for half an hour.

2. To make the filling, warm the butter and oil in a pan. Add the shallots and fry over a moderate heat for 5 minutes until softened. Stir in the garlic, and cook until fragrant.

3. Add the chicken, and then the spring onions. Cook for a couple of minutes, then sprinkle over the flour. Stir until the flour is coating the chicken, and then add the Marsala. Once it has bubbled away for a minute, add the stock, and simmer until the sauce is thick. Season with the mustard, salt, and pepper, then add the peas and turn off the heat. Transfer to a bowl and put in the fridge to cool completely.

4. Preheat the oven to 180C fan/400F/gas 6. In a bid to make your life as easy as possible (this is supposed to be lazy-day leftovers, after all, and we're already on Step 4), put a baking tray in the oven to heat up. I'm not going to suggest you blind bake the shortcrust pastry, so the heat from the hot tray will ensure that the bottom of the pie cooks evenly. Roll out the pastry to a coin-thick disc, and line a pie dish with it. Prick it all over with a fork and put it back in the fridge for half an hour.

5. Spoon the chilled filling into the pastry, paint the edge of the base with beaten egg, cover with a sheet of puff pastry, and crimp (or use a fork) to seal. Paint the top with more beaten egg, and transfer to the oven, on top of the tray. Bake for 40 minutes, until puffed and golden brown.

PASTRY
60g/¼ cup butter
120g/1 cup - 1½tbsp plain/all-purpose flour
1 egg yolk

FILLING
1tbsp butter
1tbsp groundnut oil
2 banana shallots, finely sliced
3 cloves garlic, crushed
300g/10oz leftover scraps of chicken, pulled off the bone
6 spring onions/ scallions, sliced
2tbsp plain/all-purpose flour
3tbsp Marsala
500ml/2 cups chicken stock
1tsp English mustard
Salt and black pepper
120g/1 cup frozen peas

TOPPING
1 egg
A sheet of ready-rolled puff pastry

EQUIPMENT
23cm/9in pie dish

Apricot and peach trees

He was baffled to know that apricot trees existed in, of all places,
our orchard. On late afternoons, when there was nothing to do in the
house, Mafalda would ask him to climb a ladder with a basket and
pick those fruit that were almost blushing with shame, she said [...]
I shall never forget watching him from my table as he climbed the
small ladder wearing his red bathing trunks, taking forever to
pick the ripest apricots.
Call Me By Your Name, André Aciman

I read *Call Me By Your Name* on a cold December night in
Edinburgh, my back pressed up against the radiator as cakes for
an event baked in shifts. I held my paperback in my left hand as
I whisked batter with my right, and thought about the story for
long weeks afterwards. Aciman transported me away from the
dark grey night outside, straight to the Ligurian coast, fragrant
with herbs, and bathed in August sunshine. Though the focus is
on the relationship between Elio and Oliver, the book is also the
recollection of a summer spent on the Italian Riviera. It is about
lazy, languid afternoons, about bike rides that end in scoops of
gelato, about glasses of apricot juice and soft-boiled eggs enjoyed
at the breakfast table, about the scent of rosemary in the garden.

Geographically, Liguria is a thin strip of land along the north-west
Italian coast, between the sea and the hills. The region is rich in
lush fruit and vegetables, especially in the summer. Famous for its
olive oil, and for the herbs that grow wild along the hills, it is also
home to peach and apricot trees that provide a generous bounty
in the summer. I have travelled along this coast a handful of times,
but have yet to spend more than a night or two there. I barely know
it, and I don't speak Italian, but as I closed *Call Me By Your Name*,
I felt a strong desire to get on a plane and move there.

It's relatively rare to read a book that is genuinely life-altering.
Life-enhancing, certainly, but life-altering is something else
entirely. I left Elio and Oliver, and their transformative summer
romance, wanting to be a better, braver, more open person. And,
in an impulse that will be a surprise to no one, wanting to eat plate
after plate of herb-rich, summery Italian food.

Mandilli di seta (Pasta squares with pesto)

Liguria is famed for its pesto. Wild, fragrant basil grows there in abundance, and pesto is the perfect vehicle for its uniquely peppery fragrance. You don't have to make the pasta by hand – ready-made fresh lasagna sheets are a good alternative – but if you've not done it before, I recommend giving it a go.

Serves 4

1. To make the pasta, pour the flour into a mound on your work surface. Make a well in the middle, crack in the eggs and add the olive oil. Swirl the flour into the eggs with a fork. Knead the dough for 10 minutes or so, until a shallow indent made with your finger bounces back. Cover with plastic wrap and chill for at least half an hour.

2. Meanwhile, make the pesto. Toast the pine nuts in a dry pan. Tip into a small food processor, or into a container that will fit a stab mixer. Add the basil, garlic cloves, Parmesan, and seasoning, and blitz. Add the oil, a teaspoon at a time, until the pesto is a loose sauce. Taste and season again if needed.

3. If you have a pasta machine, this next step will be relatively easy. Cut your dough into 4. Working with one piece at a time, dust in flour, roll out with a rolling pin and then run through the pasta machine settings until very thin (start with the widest and run through this a couple of times to get started). Slice into large squares (like lasagna sheets) and hang to dry. If you don't have a pasta machine, you'll need to roll it out by hand until the pasta is just slightly thicker than a playing card.

4. Bring a big pot of generously salted water to the boil and cook until al dente. This will take only minutes, so keep an eye on it. Use a mug to reserve some of the cooking water.

5. Drain the pasta, tip it back into the pot, and add the pesto. Toss through, adding a little of the cooking water to lubricate if it's feeling too dry. Serve the sheets in bowls, with some extra Parmesan alongside.

PASTA
400g/3 cups Tipo 00 flour
4 eggs (ideally ones with golden orange yolks)
1tbsp olive oil

PESTO
40g/⅓ cup pine nuts
100g/5 cups fresh basil leaves
2 cloves garlic
40g/½ cup grated Parmesan (or a vegetarian alternative)
Salt and black pepper
2tbsp olive oil

EQUIPMENT
Pasta maker (or rolling pin)
Food processor or stab mixer

Stuffed courgette flowers

COURGETTE FLOWERS
180g/¾ cup ricotta
2tbsp Parmesan (or a vegetarian alternative)
Zest of 2 lemons
10g/½ cup chopped basil leaves
10g/½ cup chopped rosemary leaves
10g/½ cup chopped oregano leaves
Salt and black pepper
6 large courgette/zucchini flowers, with the courgette still attached

BATTER
60g/½ cup cornflour/cornstarch
60g/scant ½ cup plain/all-purpose flour
½tsp baking powder
150ml/⅔ cup ice-cold fizzy water
Flaky sea salt

AND
1 litre/4¼ cups vegetable oil

I know, I know, a pot of hot oil on the hob in the middle of summer. Stay with me – these are worth it. Of course, you can make these on a slightly cooler day, but the short season of courgette flowers means you might have to put up with oil on the hob on a sunny day. You need to enjoy them when they're at their peak, and this is my absolute favourite way: filled with fresh, fragrant herbs, and salty cheese.

Serves 6

1. In a bowl, mix together the ricotta, Parmesan, lemon zest, and herbs. Taste and season. Spoon the mixture into a disposable piping bag, if you have one, or a freezer bag if not.

2. Open the petals of the flowers so that you can see inside to where the flower and courgette are connected. Snip the end of the piping bag, work the open tip into the flower, and squeeze to fill with the ricotta stuffing. Twist the petal tips together at the top, and set aside (in the fridge if you don't want to cook them immediately).

3. Put the oil in a high-sided saucepan over a moderate heat, and bring up to a temperature of 180C/355F. Whisk together the flours and baking powder in a bowl. Slowly pour in the fizzy water, trying not to let it froth too much. Whisk gently, until the ingredients are just combined – over-whisking will make the batter tough.

4. Once the oil is hot, dip the flowers, one by one, into the batter, then carefully drop them into the oil (don't crowd the pan). Once the batter is pale golden, remove them to a paper towel with a slotted spoon. Drain and cool for a couple of minutes, then season with salt, and serve.

Peach and apricot tart

If you have read *Call Me By Your Name*, you will know it would be remiss of me not to include a recipe for peaches here. It's no hardship; they're among my most beloved fruit. By the time they appear on the shelves, my hayfever has subsided, and I am already looking forward to autumn appearing. But, for the month or so when they're at their best, I'd happily live on them alone. If you have a bowlful of ripe fruit, it would be lovely used raw in this tart, with a drizzle of rosemary honey. But if your fruit is a little less yielding, do try roasting it first.

Serves 10

1. Preheat the oven to 180C fan/400F/gas 6. Slice the peaches and apricots in half, pull out the stones, and put them cut-side up in a roasting dish. Drizzle the honey over the top, along with the leaves from 2 sprigs of the rosemary. Roast for half an hour, and then cool to room temperature while you prepare the tart.

2. While the fruit is in the oven, prepare the pastry. In a food processor, blitz the flour and icing sugar with the butter, until it resembles breadcrumbs. Alternatively, you can do this with your fingertips, but this is a soft and sweet pastry – it melts easily if you have warm hands. Use the egg to bring the pastry together, then roll it into a log, and cover it with plastic wrap. Chill in the fridge for half an hour.

3. Once firm, cut into round discs. The pastry is too soft and sweet to roll out easily, especially in the summer. Press the rounds of pastry into the tart tin, right up the sides, using a wodge of pastry to push it into the corners and seal any joins. Prick the pastry all over, and return to the fridge for another half an hour, until firm. Turn up the oven to 200C fan/425F/gas 7 – your fruit should be done by now – just before you bring the pastry out of the fridge.

TOP
4 peaches
6 apricots
4tbsp honey
4 sprigs rosemary

PASTRY
250g/1¾ cups plain/all-purpose flour
100g/scant ¾ cup icing/confectioners sugar
125g/½ cup butter, cubed
1 egg

FILLING
400g/14oz ricotta
Zest of a lemon
Zest of an orange
50g/¼ cup caster/superfine sugar
1 egg

EQUIPMENT
20cm/9in loose-bottomed tart tin/pan

4. Cover the pastry with 2 sheets of plastic wrap, and pour baking beans or rice in, right up to the top of the pastry. Bake for 20 minutes, then remove the beans or rice and wrap and bake until the pastry is golden and dry to the touch (about 10 minutes).

5. Turn the oven down to 160C fan/350F/gas 4. Whisk the ingredients for the ricotta filling together. Once the pastry is cool enough to touch, spoon the filling into it and smooth off the top. Bake for 20 minutes until set.

6. Once the tart has cooled to room temperature, spoon the peaches and apricots onto the top. Tip the roasting juices into a small saucepan, and simmer with the rest of the rosemary sprigs until it is a viscous syrup. Spoon this over the fruit on the tart, and serve.

Australian Christmas

*Boxing Day had fallen on a Saturday that year, and the last of our
guests had departed on Sunday morning. It was the first time we had
had any quietude for many weeks, so in the afternoon I went out to
swing in my hammock and meditate upon things in general. Taking
with me a bountiful supply of figs, apricots, and mulberries, I laid
myself out for a deal of enjoyment in the cool dense shade under the
leafy kurrajong- and cedar-trees.*
My Brilliant Career, Miles Franklin

Like most people I know, my Christmases have always been
steeped in ritual and routine. Each year, we went to Midnight Mass,
singing carols with gusto as our sweaty thighs stuck to plastic
seats, and sneaking out after communion to eat mulberries straight
from the churchyard tree. In early December, we clipped together
a gloriously fake fir tree and we spent every Boxing Day in the
pool, clutching drinks that perspired with us in the heat. Christmas
was heat and dust – the Australia of *My Brilliant Career*, *The Magic
Pudding*, and *Seven Little Australians*. It was the smell of summer
rain falling onto hot, sticky roads. It was cooking out of doors, or
as little as possible, subsisting on tropical fruit and zingy salads.

When my stepfather woke us up each December morning with
Bing Crosby singing songs about snow and roaring fires and
roasting chestnuts, he was singing of a world that felt like a
fairy tale. Our Christmases weren't like the ones I read about in
my favourite stories – we didn't wassail through the snow like
the March sisters, or wrap scarves around our throats like Bob
Cratchit – but our rituals were comforting in their familiarity
and consistency. Instead of stuffing, bird, and roast potatoes,
our dinner plates were piled high with prawns, salads, and cold
meats. We made an 'English Christmas' concession only for my
great-grandmother's pudding; served in small slices beside the
ubiquitous white cloud of pavlova.

The meal that follows takes advantage of the best warm-weather
produce, and would work equally well as a non-Christmas meal
in the height of summer in the northern hemisphere. It's been ten
years since I have celebrated Christmas in Australia, but when
I eat food like this I think of Franklin's Sybylla Melvyn, lying in
the shade on Boxing Day with her bountiful supply of fresh fruit.

Prawn, avocado, and mango salad

1 red onion, sliced
Juice of 1 lime
400g/14oz raw shelled prawns/shrimp
2 ripe avocados
2 ripe mangoes
20g/1 cup mint leaves
20g/1 cup coriander/cilantro leaves
2 spring onions/scallions, green tops only, finely sliced

DRESSING
2tsp fish sauce
1tsp caster/superfine sugar
Juice of 1 lime
1 mild red chilli, deseeded and finely chopped
1tbsp black sesame seeds

This is my childhood summer on a plate. On hot nights, we'd pull a box of prawns out of the freezer and defrost them in the sink, relishing the feel of their cool flesh as we peeled them, before eating them on soft white bread with homemade seafood sauce and slices of avocado. This is a more grown-up, fancier version; perfect as a generous starter, on a platter in the middle of the table on Christmas Day, or for a light supper.

Serves 4 as a main or 8 as a starter

1. Put the red onion into a bowl, with the lime juice. Squash and squeeze it a little with your hands until it starts to soften.

2. Slice down the backs of the prawns, and remove the vein. Grill them on the barbeque, or in a heavy cast-iron pan, until pink and tender. Try not to leave them too long; you don't want them to be chewy.

3. Slice the flesh of the avocados and mangoes, and put in a bowl with the herbs, prawns, chopped spring onions, and the softened red onion.

4. In a separate bowl, stir together the fish sauce, caster sugar, lime juice and chilli, until the sugar is dissolved.

5. Toss the salad ingredients with the dressing. Top with sesame seeds, and serve in a salad bowl, or in a pile on a plate in front of each guest.

Passion fruit curd pavlova

In Brisbane, when it was too hot to cook, we'd buy a pavlova base from the bakery up the road, and cover it with cream and fruit at home. Happily, in England, most summer evenings are cool enough to justify having the oven on low for a meringue. This pavlova uses everything that Sybylla takes with her to eat in the shade of a tree, brought together with a sharp passion fruit curd.

Serves 8

1. Bake the meringue the night before. Preheat the oven to 150C fan/325F/gas 3. Beat the egg whites until frothy and starting to form soft peaks. Add the caster sugar a tablespoon at a time, beating until the meringue forms very stiff peaks. Don't beat it on a high speed, or you will end up overdoing it. Be patient, and keep going until the sugar has dissolved; you don't want to feel any grains if you rub a pinch of the meringue between your fingertips.

2. Line a baking sheet with parchment paper. Fold in the cream of tartar, vinegar, and salt. Spoon the meringue into a circular mound in the middle of the sheet. Flatten the top, and transfer to the oven. Bake for 90 minutes, then turn off the oven, and leave the meringue in it to cool overnight.

3. For the curd, blitz the passion fruit pulp for 5 seconds in a food processor, to loosen the seeds from the flesh. Push through a fine sieve. You should have about 80ml/⅓ cup of juice; if you don't, make up the rest with lemon juice.

4. In a heatproof bowl, whisk the juice with the sugar, whole eggs, and egg yolks. Place over a pan of simmering water and stir for about 15 minutes until thick enough to coat a spoon. Take off the heat, and whisk in the butter, a spoonful at a time. Chill in the fridge.

5. To assemble, place the meringue on a plate. Whisk the cream to soft, billowy peaks and spoon on top. Cover with about 200g/⅔ cup of the passion fruit curd. Rinse the fruit, slice, and arrange over the cream and curd. Serve immediately.

PAVLOVA
5 egg whites
250g/1¼ cups golden caster/superfine sugar
1tsp cream of tartar
1tsp white wine vinegar
A pinch of salt

PASSION FRUIT CURD
8 passion fruit
Juice of up to 2 lemons, if needed
150g/¾ cup caster/superfine sugar
2 whole eggs
2 egg yolks
125g/½ cup unsalted butter

AND
500ml/2 cups double/heavy cream
8 ripe apricots
8 ripe figs
150g/1 cup mulberries (or blackberries, if you can't get hold of them)

EQUIPMENT
Electric whisk or mixer

White sangria

150ml/⅔ cup brandy, or apple brandy

150g/¾ cup caster/superfine sugar

1 lime

1 lemon

1 peach

100g/¾ cup blackberries

A bottle of dry white wine

Ice cubes

My most beloved Christmas drink here in England is mulled wine, but it would never work for an Australian Christmas. With the heat and humidity, a very different fruity, boozy drink is called for. This fits the bill perfectly.

Makes 8 glasses

1. Pour the brandy and sugar into a jug, and stir to dissolve. Slice the lime and lemon into thin rounds, remove any seeds, then add the slices to the jug. Muddle the citrus fruit in the brandy and sugar.

2. Stone and slice the peach. Add this to the jug along with the blackberries. Pour in the wine, stir, add ice, and serve.

Holidays on the Mediterranean

*If it had been morning I could have cut through the fields and
vineyards, and before reaching home I would have fed well on
contributions from various of my friends on the way: olives, bread,
grapes, figs, ending perhaps with a short detour that would take me
through Philomena's fields, where I could be sure of ending my snack
with a crisp, pink slice of water-melon, cold as ice.*
My Family and Other Animals, Gerald Durrell

The first summer I was in England I booked a trip to Italy with
a friend from Australia. It was August and blisteringly hot; the
photos of us show shiny red noses, sweat-matted hair, and big, silly
grins. During our stay I thought often of Shakespeare's *Romeo and
Juliet* (not least as we drove through fair Verona), and of Benvolio's
musings on the impact of hot European summers:

*I pray thee, good Mercutio, let's retire.
The day is hot; the Capulets, abroad;
And if we meet we shall not 'scape a brawl,
For now, these hot days, is the mad blood stirring.*

I'm a pain to live with in the heat: moody, lazy, and 'mad of blood'.
It doesn't suit me. But during that summer, I learnt that in order
to enjoy Mediterranean heat (which is not unlike the Queensland
heat I grew up with) one must simply succumb to it. This is
difficult when you're trying to look fresh for work, but glorious if
you're on holiday. It demands downtime, to lie in the shade with
an ice-cream cone and book. It implores you to hunt out bodies
of water, trying to tempt a gentle breeze to cool your skin, and it
actively encourages you to eat outdoors in the shade of a generous
umbrella, or with bare feet dangling off rocks and into the sea.

It's the food of the Mediterranean that most makes me want to
travel, even in the hottest months. The chicken roasted with
artichokes that Marge brings to the table in *The Talented Mr Ripley*.
Brideshead Revisited's Charles and Sebastian eating a breakfast
of cool melon and prosciutto on the balcony in Venice. The crisp,
pink slice of watermelon that completes Gerald Durrell's on-the-
move feasting in *My Family and Other Animals*. It may not be my
most beloved season, but my goodness the food is good.

Grilled fish rolls

When I visited Istanbul, we found ourselves one balmy evening on the shoreline of the Bosporus. Rows of barbeques were lined with fillets of fish, destined to be stuffed into generous lengths of baguette alongside handfuls of fragrant herbs. We'd eaten in so many incredible places in Istanbul but this fish, straight off the barbeque, and eaten with our legs dangling over the side of the pier, was my favourite meal of the trip.

Serves 2

1. Sprinkle the pul biber and dried mint over both sides of the fillets, rub with oil, and season the skin with pepper and salt. Fry the fish in a pan over a high heat – skin-side down first, until it is crisp and golden and you can easily lift it up, and then for a couple of minutes on the other side. Turn off the heat.

2. Meanwhile, pour the lemon juice over the onion, add a generous pinch of salt, and squeeze with your hands, until the onion softens. Set aside. Toss the herbs together.

3. Slice the baguette open, and drizzle with olive oil. Divide the herbs and the onion between the rolls, and put the hot fish inside, breaking the fillets in half if you need to. Eat immediately.

FISH
1tsp pul biber (mild Turkish chilli flakes)
1tsp dried mint
2 fillets sea bass or mackerel
1tbsp olive oil
Salt and black pepper

ROLL
Juice of 1 lemon
1 brown onion, sliced
A generous pinch of salt
A handful of mint leaves
A handful of parsley leaves
A handful of coriander/ cilantro leaves
Fronds from 4 stalks of dill
1 baguette
1tbsp olive oil

Chicken with artichokes and potatoes

600g/1lb 5oz baby
potatoes
1 whole chicken (about
1.8kg/4lbs)
1 brown onion
4 cloves garlic
12 pieces marinated
artichoke
10 sprigs thyme
A generous drizzle of
olive oil
Salt and black pepper
1 lemon
40g/2½tbsp butter,
softened

There is nothing I find as mouth-watering as the smell of
a chicken cooking in the oven. This is a take on the dish
Marge Sherwood serves to Tom Ripley when he arrives out
of the blue at the house she shares with Dickie. The story
quickly becomes a tense thriller, but in these early pages,
Tom is welcomed into their home with a chicken dinner.
What a welcome.

Serves 6 (or fewer, with generous leftovers)

1. Par-boil the potatoes for 10 minutes until tender, but not
soft. Drain and set aside.

2. Prepare the chicken. Place it breast-side down and cut
down either side of the backbone; kitchen scissors are good
for this. Remove the backbone (keep it for making stock),
and flip the chicken over. Spread it out and press down on
the breastbone with the heel of your hand to flatten.

3. Slice the onion and place in the bottom of a roasting dish.
Add the garlic cloves, whole. Place the chicken into the
dish, breast-side up.

4. Add the potatoes and artichokes. Poke the thyme stalks
in between the potatoes. Drizzle them with olive oil and
season with salt, pepper and a big squeeze of lemon.

5. Rub the butter over the chicken skin, and season.
Transfer the dish to an oven preheated to 200C fan/425F/
gas 7. Alternatively, cover it with plastic wrap, and store in
the fridge for up to a day.

6. Roast the chicken for 45 minutes. To test if it is done,
poke a skewer into the biggest part of the thigh; the juices
should run clear. Remove from the oven, allow the chicken
to rest for 10 minutes under foil, then carve and serve with
the potatoes and artichokes. A crisp green salad alongside
is ideal.

Watermelon granita

After re-reading Gerald Durrell's *My Family and Other Animals*, I found myself craving slices of watermelon. I've always loved the fruit, relishing the chance to spit the seeds at my sister almost as much as I did the eating of it. The idea of the watery flesh, 'cold as ice', cooling us down from the inside out on impossibly warm afternoons was just what the summer called for. I found myself making batches and batches of this during the heatwave of 2018 – the only thing that managed to get my core temperature down on those scorchingly hot days.

Makes enough for 8

1. Slice the watermelon flesh away from the skin, and chop it into chunks, taking all the seeds out as you go.

2. Put the watermelon, sugar, chilli, lime juice, and salt in the blender, and blitz until they have formed a smooth purée.

3. Pour into a dish, cover, and place in the freezer. After an hour, scrape the frozen bits into the centre, break it all up with a fork, and return to the freezer.

4. After around 4 hours (depending on how shallow your dish was) you'll have granita. Scrape it with a fork, and serve the shavings in a glass.

A 1.5kg/3lb 5oz watermelon*
125g/⅔ cup caster/superfine sugar
1tsp chilli flakes
Juice of 2 limes
1tsp flaky salt

EQUIPMENT
Blender

* If you can get your hands on a seedless watermelon, it's a dream here: this recipe will become the work of moments.

More books for those sweltering, languid, lazy summer months...

Shop for flowers, and then wander the streets of central London with *Mrs Dalloway*. Suffer through a swelteringly hot New Orleans day with *A Streetcar Named Desire*'s Blanche and Stella. Lay out a picnic blanket and feast on strawberries in the long grass with *Emma* and Mr Knightley. Lie awake through the long summer nights, waiting for the grandfather clock to strike, then stumble down the stairs and into *Tom's Midnight Garden*. Play the voyeur with the boys across the road in *The Virgin Suicides*, and find yourself obsessed with the lives of the captivating Lisbon sisters. Take a journey up *Cannery Row*, stopping in at the grocer's on your way. Spend some time (though not too much) on the French Riviera, in the company of *Bonjour Tristesse*'s inimitable Cécile. Spend a sweltering summer on the Italian coast with Elena in *The Story of a New Name*. Join a centipede, a spider, a ladybird, and (most importantly) *James and the Giant Peach* and help yourself to a handful of ripe, delicious fruit. Solve the murder of Aristide Leonides by poking your nose into the rooms of the *Crooked House*. Follow *Madam, Will You Talk?*'s Charity Selborne, and her friend Louise, on a holiday to Provence that turns out to be slightly more of an adventure than they anticipated. Battle against racism and injustice, and eat macaroni cheese alongside sixteen-year-old Starr Carter in *The Hate U Give*. Spend a summer in the *Wild* with Cheryl, dreaming of Snapple and peaches, while hiking the Pacific Crest Trail.

When the leaves start to turn

When the leaves start to turn

I'm so glad I live in a world where there are Octobers.
Anne of Green Gables, L. M. Montgomery

I breathe a heartfelt and genuine sigh of relief when autumn arrives each year. Growing up, I longed for it; it meant the end of sweltering Australian summer days, and the respite that the all too brief autumn and winter brought with them. Autumn heralded the arrival of my birthday, the unpacking of the school blazer that felt reassuringly heavy around my shoulders, and evenings indoors on the sofa, rather than outside on the deck. But autumn in the northern hemisphere promised so much more. Though the mornings were brisk, and the evenings chilly, Brisbane stays resolutely green, whatever the season. I longed for the opening sequence of *You've Got Mail*: bouquets of freshly sharpened pencils and pumpkins being sold on street corners. I wanted to see the leaves of the Whomping Willow turning in the grounds of Hogwarts, to walk with Danny and William through Hazell's Wood on the hunt for pheasants, watching as autumn changed the world around me.

My first autumn in England brought with it my first theatre job, an internship in a tiny pub theatre in Islington. I sat on the top deck of the bus each morning and observed my fellow commuters change as the weather did; scarves and coats were brought out of storage, and turned the sartorial palette of London into a monochrome of blacks and greys at odds with the glorious colours of the trees. I read John Irving and Stephen King novels on my commute, and thought of one day visiting New England in the fall. I saved up and bought a postbox red coat, and went out of my way to kick the leaves that carpeted the footpaths of Upper Street, before they could be swept away by the winds.

On the first day of November in 2009, the trees in London seemed to come to a sudden and communal realization: they had mere weeks left of autumn, and the time to drop their leaves had nearly passed them by. I walked from the station in High Street Kensington to my tutoring job that evening, shin-deep in leaves, dreaming of returning

home to a pot of chilli, and to the last of the tea loaf I'd left under a cloth. It is my first memory of feeling truly at home in England, of knowing that this was the place I was meant to be.

Ten years later, I still experience the same frisson of excitement when summer begins to recede. As the leaves begin to flame around the edges, acquiring the colours of a Gryffindor crest, as apples arrive in wooden crates at the farmers' markets, as the cooler evenings gently suggest dinners indoors with dear friends, my mood changes dramatically. Plans for long alfresco lunches and the bright salads of summer are pushed from my mind, and I make countless soups, bake loaves of bread, and explore the game birds, which arrive in the butcher's window with such reliable timing I could set my calendar by them. I hibernate, happily, and embrace the chance to spend more time indoors. I assemble a pile of 'college' and 'back to school' books on my bedside table and delve into eerie old favourites by Shirley Jackson and Mary Shelley, books that just wouldn't feel right in summer. As the year marches on, and the sound of fireworks echoes almost nightly in the sky, you can reliably find me in a pair of bed socks, book in hand, by the stove.

Tuck boxes

'Good girl,' said her mother, shutting down the lid of the trunk. 'Now look Elizabeth – this is your tuck-box. I've put a tin of toffees in, a big chocolate cake, a tin of shortbread, and a large pot of blackcurrant jam. That's all I can get in. But I think it's enough, don't you?'
The Naughtiest Girl Again, Enid Blyton

When I was eight, lying sideways on the bottom bunk with my head dangling over the edge, this line had an indelible impact. With my primary school an easy walking distance up the road, the idea of heading off to boarding school was already foreign enough. But the thought of a box, with my name stamped onto it, filled with cakes, sweets, and biscuits, was almost too much to bear. I'd experienced a lifetime of packed lunches – miniature tuckboxes – but they contained a lunch for me alone: a cheese and salad sandwich, a banana, and a frozen juice box to keep it all cool. I wanted pots of jam, tins of biscuits, and bags of toffees and fudge to share with my friends.

By the time I started reading Harry Potter a couple of years later, I was obsessed. Though I adored my family, I thought it deeply unfair that heading off to boarding school, to sleep in dorms, do homework around a fire, and have secret midnight feasts, was going to be denied me. I didn't really find my crowd at school until my final years, but was convinced that being forced to all live together at school would turn enemies into the dearest friends, like the escaped mountain troll did for my favourite Hogwarts trio.

My obsession with boarding-school tuck boxes has remained into adulthood; I love sending treats through the post to someone who might be in need of them. It's unlikely to be a grateful schoolgirl on the receiving end, but instead a sleep-deprived new mum, or a friend who's just moved into a new home. There's something about it that feels undeniably 'old school'. It's a joy to bake or make something (ideally with a long shelf life), wrap it up, and walk it down to the Post Office. So much of our correspondence happens now thanks to the wonder of the Internet, and though it allows me to stay in contact with my family, the feeling of being the recipient of a parcel in the post is impossible to replicate. It's a service worth celebrating with a date cake.

Back-to-school jam

500g/4⅓ cups mix of blackcurrants, redcurrants, and blackberries – anything you can collect from the hedgerows at the end of the summer
500g/2½ cups preserving sugar*
Juice of 2 lemons
4 bay leaves

EQUIPMENT
Medium-sized non-reactive saucepan

*Currants are naturally high in pectin, so you don't have to use a preserving sugar for this recipe. Preserving sugar will melt more evenly and there will be less scum to scrape off, but you can use granulated sugar if you have some in the cupboard – this is supposed to be an easy jam/jelly.

Thanks to their many tiny seeds, I've always felt that blackcurrants are better when mixed together with other berries – especially others you can pull from the hedgerows in the last weeks of summer. Fresh blackcurrants are generally quite expensive in supermarkets, so keep your eyes peeled at farmers' markets when they're in season, find a friend with a shrub in their garden, or use frozen berries instead.

Makes enough to fill 3 x 300g/10oz jars

1. First, put a couple of plates in the freezer. Wash the fruit, if fresh, and tip it into a stainless-steel or enamel saucepan. Stir the sugar through it, add the lemon juice, and squash the fruit so it gives off some of its juice. Add the bay leaves.

2. Bring to a simmer over a low heat. Stir regularly to ensure the jam doesn't catch on the bottom. Skim any scum from the top as it cooks.

3. After 20 minutes, turn off the heat. Take a plate out of the freezer and put a spoonful of the jam onto it. Count to 10 and push the jam; if it wrinkles, rather than staying liquid, it is ready. If not, put it back over the heat. Once at setting point, pour the jam, along with the bay leaves, into sterilized jars (see p 158). Store for months, or eat as soon as it has cooled down a little, on warm bread, with butter.

Salted buttermilk fudge

I'm not generally an enthusiastic lover of fudge. Hagrid seems to be a fan in *Harry Potter and the Chamber of Secrets*, but the only use the others find for it is to stick the bloodhound Fang's teeth together to keep him quiet. This confirmed all my fudge-related prejudice; it's oversweet, chewy, and cloying. When a friend requested I make her some, I was reluctant, but I had a bit of buttermilk in the fridge and used it in place of the usual sickly condensed milk. Though it's still sweet enough to give you a bit of a sugar rush, the salt and the sour buttermilk cut through it, making a more rounded, grown-up fudge that's far too easy to eat in alarmingly large quantities.

Makes a generous box – about 24 pieces

1. Line a tin with parchment paper. Stir the caster sugar and buttermilk together in a saucepan. Add the butter and the golden syrup, and place over a moderate heat. Stir only once the sugar has melted, so that it does not crystallize.

2. Simmer the mixture until it reaches 116C/240F. Turn off the heat, leave for 5 minutes, then add the vanilla and the salt. Beat the fudge vigorously with a wooden spoon, until it is dull rather than shiny.

3. Pour into the tin, and leave for a couple of hours to harden. Slice into squares, and store in an airtight container.

430g/heaped 2 cups caster/superfine sugar
260ml/generous 1 cup buttermilk
15g/1 tbsp butter
1tbsp golden syrup
1tsp vanilla extract
A generous pinch of flaky salt

EQUIPMENT
Small roasting dish, cake tin/pan or tray (about 25 x 15cm/10 x 6in)

Date and walnut loaf

1tsp bicarbonate of soda/baking soda

225g/1⅓ cups chopped dates

150ml/⅔ cup boiling water

30g/2 tbsp butter

85g/scant ½ cup light brown sugar

45ml/3 tbsp golden syrup

1 egg

225g/1¾ cups plain/all-purpose flour

1tsp baking powder

A pinch of salt

50g/⅓ cup shelled walnut halves

This is 'Molly's cake', a recipe that has come to me through my adopted English family – a cake that was made with some regularity by matriarch Molly, and now by her daughter Anne. It's robust and forgiving, and best served in thick slices. Ideal for wrapping up and sending across the country in a tuck box.

Makes 10 slices

1. Preheat the oven to 160C fan/350F/gas 4. Sprinkle the bicarb over the dates, and then pour over the boiling water.

2. Cream together the butter, sugar, and golden syrup until light. Beat in the egg. Fold in the flour, baking powder, and salt, and then stir in the walnuts and dates, along with their soaking liquid.

3. Spoon the batter into a lined loaf tin and bake for an hour, until a skewer inserted in the centre comes out clean. Serve in slices, spread thickly with good salted butter.

Buchteln

Though these are undoubtedly best eaten the day they are baked, I wanted to include them in this chapter. They're what the girls in the first of the Chalet School books feast upon on Sunday mornings, with big mugs of milky coffee. They are to be packed at the top of your tuck box, ready to be brought out as soon as the train pulls away from the station.

Serves 8

1. Put the milk and 75g/5tbsp of the butter into a saucepan, and warm over a low heat until the butter melts. Remove from the heat, and leave to cool until lukewarm. Whisk in the sugar, then the yeast. Add the egg and egg yolk.

2. Put the flours and salt in a mixing bowl. Tip in the liquid mixture, and bring together into a dough using a wooden spoon. Knead for 10 minutes until it is smooth, and bounces back when you prod it. The dough should be sticky, but do add a little flour to help your kneading if needed.

3. Wash out the mixing bowl, then grease it with a little butter and place the dough back in. Cover and leave to proof for an hour, until doubled in size.

4. Weigh the dough, and cut it into 8 equal pieces. Flatten each (not too thinly in the centre, or the dough might split), place a teaspoon of plum jam into the centre, and pull the edges up. Pinch them together, then flip the ball and roll it on the work surface. Place each roll in a greased oven dish, giving them a little space to swell. Allow to proof for around 40 minutes – long enough to let the rolls join up. They should bounce back when prodded gently.

5. Preheat the oven to 180C fan/400F/gas 6. Melt the rest of the butter, brush it over the rolls, and bake for 20–25 minutes, until risen and golden. Dust with icing sugar, and serve with honey, and sweet, milky coffee.

150ml/⅔ cup milk
100g/7tbsp unsalted butter
50g/¼ cup golden caster/superfine sugar
15g/3tsp fresh yeast (or 5g/1½tsp easy-action yeast)
1 egg
1 egg yolk
175g/1 cup plain/all-purpose flour
150g/1⅓ cups strong white bread flour
A pinch of salt
60g/¼ cup plum jam/jelly
1tbsp icing/confectioner's sugar

The hunt for the perfect apple

Never to be forgotten, that first long secret drink of golden fire, juice of those valleys and of that time, wine of the wild orchards, of russet summer, of plump red apples, and Rosie's burning cheeks. Never to be forgotten, or ever tasted again...
Cider with Rosie, Laurie Lee

The humble apple is common in mythology, appearing in stories from Norse, Greek, Chinese, and Germanic traditions. Though the fruit pulled from the tree in the Garden of Eden is not identified in the Book of Genesis, it is commonly depicted as an apple. A poisoned apple sends Snow White into a deep sleep, and a well-timed apple dropping from a tree was (probably not really) responsible for inspiring Isaac Newton's Law of Universal Gravitation. The Beatles named their record label after it and, on returning from a trip to an Oregon orchard in the mid-1980s, Steve Jobs suggested the name Apple Computers to Steve Wozniak.

We know what it is to be a bad apple, to visit the Big Apple, and how it feels to be the apple of someone's eye. We are aware that apples never fall far from the tree, that they're fundamentally different to oranges, and that, in the end, she'll be apples. And yet, despite their ubiquity, the apples we most often lay our hands on are such a narrow representation of the variety on offer.

When I first arrived in the UK, I was surprised to find familiar antipodean apples in the supermarkets. They're vibrant, and shiny, and are, visually, the Platonic ideal, but after a childhood of them in my lunchbox, I was hoping for something new. Though there are over 7,500 varieties of apple growing around the world, most supermarkets only offer a handful of them. I started to ask friends and family about their favourites, lingering by the apple stalls at farmers' markets hoping for a taste. I fell hard for an Ashmead's Kernel one autumn, picked for me by my friend Anna, who was working at an orchard. I live in her house now, in the Cotswolds (mere miles from Laurie Lee's old place), and she's planted a tree in her back garden that should bear fruit in a year or two. I'm so looking forward to the year we gather up armfuls of apples. I can't imagine autumn without them.

Cider apple jelly

1.5kg/3lb 5oz apples
(a mixture of varieties
is absolutely grand)
Up to 500g/2½ cups
preserving sugar*
Up to 500ml/2 cups dry
apple cider
Juice of 2 lemons

EQUIPMENT
A piece of muslin/
cheesecloth

* Apples do have
pectin in them, so you
don't need jam sugar
to make the jelly set.
I would recommend
using preserving sugar
rather than a regular
granulated, though;
the larger crystals
mean that it melts more
evenly and remains
clearer. In a jelly, clear
and bright and with a
tendency to catch the
late-afternoon sun,
it really will make a
difference.

When I think of apple cider I think of Laurie Lee's *Cider with Rosie*, and of Gloucestershire in autumn, the place I have now made my home. Looking out of my bedroom window, I lose count of the apple trees I can see. At this time of year, there are piles of their colourful fruit in the markets, and my neighbours drop round with bagfuls from their trees. When the fruit bowl is overflowing I make this jelly, a dream accompaniment for cheese, meat, delicious spread on toast, or eaten straight from the jar with a spoon.

Makes enough to fill 2 x 500ml/17oz jars

1. Chop the apples roughly, and place them (cores and all) into a large saucepan. Cover with 1¼ litres/5 cups of water. Place over a moderate heat, and bring to a simmer. Cook until soft and pulpy.

2. Strain through a piece of fine muslin. Don't try and force them through, or your jelly will end up cloudy. Let the clear juice drip through over a good few hours, or overnight.

3. Weigh the apple juice, and put in a saucepan with the same weight of sugar. Add the same amount of apple cider (500ml/2 cups cider for 500ml/2 cups apple juice), and the lemon juice.

4. Bring the jelly to a simmer, skimming the surface of any scum that forms. The jelly will reach setting point around 105C/220F, but if you don't have a thermometer, you can test it on an ice-cold plate. After it has simmered for around 15 minutes, turn off the heat, drop a little mixture on the plate, count to 10, and then nudge it with your finger. If it wrinkles, it's ready. If your finger draws a line straight through it, turn the heat back on and simmer for a little longer.

5. Pour the jelly into sterilized jars (see p. 158) and seal. It will keep for 6 months; once you have opened the jar, keep the jelly in the fridge and use within a few weeks.

Apple, fennel, celeriac, and radicchio salad

Make sure you leave this salad for when you have a little time – shaving or thinly slicing the vegetables does slow things down. That said, there's barely any cooking involved, so it's not going to compete with anything in the oven or on the hob. This is good alongside roast pork or lamb, or as something sharp and crisp beside a pie or stew.

Serves 8

1. Peel apart the radicchio leaves, give them a rinse and slice finely. Peel the celeriac with a knife, and then cut into thin strips with a vegetable peeler, or mandoline. Slice the base and fronds off the fennel, then cut lengthways into thin slices. Slice your apples through the core, into thin rounds. Remove the pips. If you're serving the salad immediately, don't worry too much about anything browning. However, if you're taking mandoline slicing slowly (which I'd very much recommend), drop the slices into a bowl of icy water. Drain everything and pat dry with paper towels before dressing.

2. To make the dressing, whisk together the cider vinegar and mustard, then slowly whisk in the oil. Season with salt and pepper. Add the salad ingredients, and toss together.

3. Toast the fennel seeds in a dry frying pan over a moderate heat. Once fragrant, tip them into a mortar and pestle and bash them around a bit. In the same pan, toast the hazelnuts, then chop roughly.

4. Top the salad with the fennel seeds, hazelnuts, and pale green fennel fronds from the bulb.

SALAD
1 head radicchio
½ celeriac/celery root
1 bulb fennel
2 crisp eating apples
1tbsp fennel seeds
50g/scant ⅓ cup hazelnuts

DRESSING
1tsp cider vinegar
1tsp hot English mustard
1tbsp rapeseed/canola oil
Salt and black pepper

Apple and tarragon cake

CAKE

2 large cooking apples, like Bramleys
150g/⅔ cup butter
150g/¾ cup light brown sugar
3 eggs
150g/1½ cups ground almonds
2tsp baking powder
100g/¾ cup plain/all-purpose flour
1tbsp finely chopped tarragon leaves
A pinch of salt

TOPPING

1 crisp eating apple, sliced very finely through the core
A pinch of light brown sugar

EQUIPMENT

20cm/8in round cake tin/pan

This is a dense, moist cake for an autumn afternoon. It works gloriously well with a pot of strong tea. You might more commonly expect to find tarragon with fish or chicken, or in a Béarnaise sauce, but its warm flavour, with hints of anise and vanilla, works wonderfully alongside apples too.

Serves 10–12

1. Preheat the oven to 150C fan/325F/gas 3. Grease and line the cake tin. Peel and core the cooking apples, chop into chunks, and place in a small saucepan with a splash of water. Bring to a simmer over a low heat, and cook until the apples break down.

2. Meanwhile, beat the butter and sugar until light and creamy. Whisk the eggs into the mix, one at a time, and then fold in the almonds, baking powder, flour, and tarragon.

3. Spoon the batter into the cake tin, then arrange the slices of eating apple over the top, and sprinkle with sugar. Bake for an hour and a half, until the cake is risen and golden brown, and a skewer inserted in the middle comes out clean.

4. Cool in the cake tin for 10 minutes, and then on a rack. Serve still warm, or at room temperature, with a spoonful of sour cream.

Rosemary tarte tatin

Sheet of ready-rolled
puff pastry
3 crisp eating apples
120g/heaped ½ cup
caster/superfine sugar
60g/¼ cup butter
1 sprig rosemary, leaves
finely chopped

This dessert is deceptively simple; a breeze to put together, and achievable for a mid-week supper. You can make puff pastry, if you like, but – honestly – I'm not sure it's worth it. The supermarket stuff is perfect, and you'll mostly taste the apples and caramel anyway.

Serves 4 (generously)

1. Preheat the oven to 180C fan/400F/gas 6. Line the base of a pie dish with parchment paper. Cut a disc of pastry that is 1cm/½in wider than your dish, prick it with a fork a handful of times, and place in the fridge.

2. Peel the apples, then cut into quarters and remove the core. Slice carefully into the rounded side, like you're preparing Hasselback potatoes, being careful not to cut right through.

3. Tip the sugar into a saucepan and melt over a medium heat until it's a rich, amber colour. Remove from the heat and whisk in the butter. Tip into the pie dish, and add the rosemary. Arrange the apples, 'Hasselback'-side down in the caramel. Bake for 20 minutes.

4. Remove the dish from the oven and increase the heat to 200C fan/425F/gas 7. Being very careful not to touch the caramel, place the chilled pastry disc over the apples, and use a knife or a spatula to tuck the edges in. Return to the oven and bake for 25 minutes, until the pastry is puffed and a deep golden brown.

5. Remove the tarte tatin from the oven and cool for 5 minutes. Place a board or serving plate over the top of the dish, and (holding it all firmly in place) quickly and confidently invert the dish, so that the pastry is on the bottom. Watch out for any hot caramel that might escape. Serve immediately with crème fraîche.

Game season

It was a cold meat pie. The meat was pink and tender with no fat or gristle in it, and there were hard-boiled eggs buried like treasures in several different places. The taste was absolutely fabulous. When I had finished the first slice, I cut another and ate that too.
Danny, the Champion of the World, Roald Dahl

As a child, if I could have chosen a single book to step straight into, it would have been *Danny, the Champion of the World*. The prospect of walking with William and Danny through the woods at dusk, fallen leaves underfoot, shaped my expectations of autumn in England. My first autumn in London was a joy, but it wasn't until I boarded a Megabus to the Cotswolds that I finally saw how breathtaking it could be. I started travelling down every month or so, the weeks spent in London in between ensuring that the seasonal changes were even more apparent. Each time I returned, the village looked like a different place: the verdant green deepening into shades of red and gold, before the trees dropped their leaves entirely.

Danny, the Champion of the World couldn't be set in any other season. I can imagine the happy spring and summer days that they spend in the caravan; Danny and William working together outdoors on the cars, and walking for hours through the countryside on sunny days. But it is in autumn that the pheasants are in season, and when William can sneak off in the middle of the night to test his newest poaching technique in Hazell's Wood.

When I thought of Mr Hazell's estate, I imagined his wood as a mere hill, with a few trees for the poachers to hide behind. And then, a few years ago, I spent a handful of Sundays catering on an estate in Wiltshire. It meant long days on my own, stomping through leaves in search of apples and handfuls of fresh herbs from the kitchen garden. The estate was home to pheasants who cut boldly across my path, and deer spotted in the distance (or, more frequently, as bags of venison sausages in the freezer). This place was enormous, two miles or more, from one end to the other. I was overwhelmed by the sheer scope of it. I thought of Danny, running through the trees in the dead of night, searching for his father – no wonder he devoured a whole pork pie the next afternoon.

Pork pie

This is Danny's famous pork pie, the one that has been imprinted on my imagination since childhood. Looking at Quentin Blake's line drawings, I could taste the whole thing: the rich pastry, the spiced pork, the large boiled eggs. I didn't try a pork pie until my twenties, but I knew exactly what I wanted from it, long before I'd had a taste.

Makes an enormous pork pie, for 10 or more

1. First, prepare the jelly. Put all the ingredients into a medium pan with 1 litre/4½ cups of water. Cover, and simmer for 2 hours.

2. To make the pastry, put the flours and salt into a bowl. Rub the butter into the flour, until the mixture resembles fine breadcrumbs. Put the lard into a jug or heatproof bowl (be careful with this bit; getting splashed with hot fat is particularly painful), and pour over the boiling water. Stir to melt the lard, and then pour over the flour. Mix with a metal knife until it's cool enough to touch, then bring it together with your hands. Leave it to cool in the bowl.

3. Reserve a quarter of the pastry for the pie lid, and roll the rest out into a disc a bit thicker than 5mm/¼in. Don't go too thin here, or you risk leaks later. Grease and line the base and sides of a loose-bottomed cake tin with parchment paper, and lower the pastry in. It's lovely, easy pastry to work with; tears can be patched up, and it won't protest at being pushed about a bit. Push the pastry right into the edge of the tin, and ease it up the sides, making sure the top edge is straight.

4. Next, prepare the filling. I'm not going to lie; this is a lot of meat to chop. Your butcher might do it, if you're lucky, but when that's not possible, I prescribe an audiobook and a quiet, rainy afternoon. Dice the shoulder and belly into 5mm/¼in cubes, and finely chop the bacon. Place into a large mixing bowl, and season with the mace, pepper, salt, sage, and thyme.

JELLY
2 pig trotters
1 brown onion
1 medium carrot
1 stalk celery
10 black peppercorns
3 bay leaves

PASTRY
280g/2 cups + 2tbsp plain/all-purpose flour
280g/2 cups strong white bread flour
A pinch of salt
90g/6tbsp butter
130g/½ cup lard
150ml/⅔ cup boiling water

FILLING
750g/1lb 10oz pork shoulder
500g/1lb 2oz pork belly, rind removed
300g/10oz streaky bacon
1tsp ground mace
2tsp ground white pepper
1tsp salt
20g/1 cup sage leaves, chopped
Leaves from 6 sprigs thyme
8 eggs

TO FINISH
2 eggs, beaten

EQUIPMENT
20cm/8in loose-bottomed cake tin/pan

5. Preheat the oven to 180C fan/400F/gas 6. Boil the eggs. This is one of the rare times I'm going to recommend you hard boil them. Bring a pan of water to the boil, lower the eggs in carefully (on a spoon so they don't crack), and set a timer for 9 minutes. Run the eggs under cold water, crack them all over, and then peel carefully.

6. Put a third of the pork mixture into the base of the pie. Arrange the eggs in a circle on top of the pork, and then pack in the rest of the meat. If it domes a little in the middle, that's fine, but make sure you have 1cm/½in of pastry at the top of the pie edges to work with.

7. Roll out the final portion of pastry, so that it's about 22cm/8½in in diameter. Wet the top centimetre of the pastry in the tin, and then lower in the lid. Seal the edges, allowing the lid to sit below the top edges, and crimp it closed. Cut a small hole in the top.

8. Transfer the pie to the oven for 30 minutes, and then reduce the heat to 160C fan/350F/gas 4, and bake for a further hour and 40 minutes. Remove from the oven and allow it to rest in the tin for a couple of minutes, then remove the sides of the tin, and carefully place the pie on a baking sheet. Paint the top and sides with beaten egg, and place back in the oven for a final half-hour.

9. Remove the pie from the oven, and allow it to sit for 10 minutes. Strain the trotter stock for the jelly, and pour it slowly into the hole at the top of the pie. Once you've poured half in, leave it to stand for an hour or so before pouring in the rest.

10. Store the pie in the fridge overnight to allow the jelly time to set. Serve in generous slices the next day, with a spoonful of the piccalilli from last winter (p. 32, if you have any left).

Potted pheasant and pickled radishes

POTTED PHEASANT

200g/7oz pork belly, rind removed

2 pheasants, plucked and ready for the oven

3 shallots, sliced

6 cloves garlic, peeled and crushed

5 bay leaves

1tbsp ground white pepper

120g/½ cup butter

200ml/generous ¾ cup vermouth

10 sage leaves, chopped

PICKLED RADISHES

200ml/generous ¾ cup cider vinegar

2tsp salt

1tbsp caster/superfine sugar

10 black peppercorns

1tbsp mustard seeds

1tbsp coriander seeds

16 unblemished radishes, finely sliced

TO SERVE

Good butter

Sourdough

Pheasant has a tendency to dry out if you don't look after it but here, alongside fatty pork and plenty of butter, you'll be at no risk of that. Start a dinner party with some pots of this in the middle of the table, and provide some good bread and butter for everyone to spoon it liberally onto. This isn't the way William and Danny would have eaten it, I know, but I think they'd enjoy it nonetheless.

Serves 8

1. Preheat the oven to 150C fan/325F/gas 3. Score the pork belly and place it into a roasting dish. Place both pheasants, breast-side down, on top of it. Add the shallots, garlic, and bay leaves, crushing them lightly in your hands to release their flavour. Sprinkle over the white pepper. Cut the butter into thin slices, and use it to cover the pheasants. Pour the vermouth around the birds, then tightly seal the dish with foil, and place in the oven.

2. Roast for at least 3 hours, checking occasionally to ensure the birds are not drying out. Add a splash of water, or vermouth, if they are. Continue cooking until the leg meat pulls apart with gentle pressure from a fork.

3. While the birds are roasting, prepare the radishes. Simmer the vinegar and seasonings in a saucepan for 10 minutes, then pour over the radishes. They'll be ready to eat after half an hour, or will keep in the fridge for 2 weeks, becoming softer and sharper as time goes on.

4. Allow the pheasants to cool a little, then place in a bowl and strip them of their meat, removing all the bones and gristle. Pull the pork apart, and add this to the bowl. Strain the liquid left in the roasting dish into a saucepan, and simmer until reduced by half. Lubricate the meat with this buttery, spiced liquid, mixing the chopped sage leaves through, then pack into a sterilized jar (see p. 158). If you're going to eat it within the next 24 hours, you can store it like this. Alternatively, it will keep for a few days in the fridge, with a layer of melted butter poured over the top. Serve spread thickly onto chewy sourdough.

When the leaves start to turn

Oatcakes and smoked trout

William is far from the only one in the village with a proclivity for poaching. For the local doctor, it's trout: lying on the riverbank, reaching into the water and tickling the bellies of the fish, then pulling them out with an expert hand. I adore trout, even more so when it's been smoked. It's lovely here served with homemade oatcakes.

Makes at least 40

1. Preheat the oven to 160C fan/350F/gas 4. Blitz the oats in a food processor until they're the texture of fine breadcrumbs. Add the salt. Put the butter in a jug and pour the boiling water over the top so it melts.

2. Pour the liquid over the oats, and mix with a wooden spoon until the mixture comes together. Roll clumps of the dough out to 2mm/¹⁄₁₆in thick, using the flour so it doesn't stick to your work surface. Cut out small discs and place onto a lined baking sheet. Bake for 15–20 minutes, until golden brown at the edges. Transfer to a cooling rack.

3. Blitz the trout fillets with the horseradish, cream cheese, and lemon juice until smooth. Taste and season with the cayenne, and salt and pepper. Spoon into a serving dish and top with some dill fronds. Serve with the oatcakes.

OATCAKES
300g/3 cups porridge oats
1tsp salt
30g/2tbsp butter
125ml/½ cup boiling water
30g/3⅔tbsp plain/all-purpose flour

TROUT PÂTÉ
2 smoked trout fillets
2tbsp grated horseradish
100g/scant ½ cup cream cheese
2tbsp lemon juice
A pinch of cayenne pepper
Salt and black pepper

TO SERVE
Dill fronds

EQUIPMENT
4cm/1½in biscuit/cookie cutter
Food processor

Welsh cakes

250g/1¾ cups + 2tbsp plain/all-purpose flour
2tbsp golden caster/superfine sugar
2½tsp baking powder
125g/½ cup butter, cubed
75g/½ cup raisins
1 egg
2tbsp milk

I like to picture William and Danny using their leftover raisins (the ones not filled with sleeping powder) to make Welsh cakes on their caravan's hotplate. You need little more than a bowl, a fork, and a glass to put these together: eminently achievable with their limited space in the caravan, and perfect in your pocket when you're heading off for a walk in the woods.

Makes around 16

1. Mix the flour, sugar and baking powder together in a bowl. Rub the cold butter through the flour with your fingertips until the mixture resembles breadcrumbs. Add the raisins and stir through.

2. Make a well in the centre of the mixture and add the egg and milk. Beat them together slightly with the fork, then slowly start bringing the flour mixture into the liquid. Continue until all flour is incorporated and you have a rich dough. Don't over-mix – stop when the mixture has just come together.

3. Lightly flour your work surface and flatten the dough with your hands (there's no need to be too neat) until it is a consistent height – about 3cm/1¼in thick. Flour the rim of a glass and cut out rounds of the dough. Repeat until the dough is used up. You can form the final cake by hand.

4. Heat a cast-iron or non-stick pan over a medium-low heat until it's too warm to hold your hand over. Place the Welsh cakes in the pan, giving them a bit of space to ensure that you can easily flip them. When they have browned underneath (around 4 minutes), flip them over and cook for a further 4 minutes. Remove from the pan, sprinkle with sugar and set aside while you cook the rest. These are best eaten warm, though they're not bad the next day, toasted and spread liberally with butter and jam.

The end of the world as we know it

Jeevan moved quickly through the store while Hua spoke. Another case of water – Jeevan was under the impression that one can never have too much – and then cans and cans of food, all the tuna and beans and soup on the shelf, pasta, anything that looked like it might last a while.
Station Eleven, Emily St. John Mandel

At the end of the world, even when all else is lost, we can't avoid the imperative to eat. In all my favourite dystopian fiction, there is a strong focus placed on food. The Man and his Son spend their journey down *The Road* pulling open cupboards in abandoned houses, searching for tins. When Jeevan is warned about the Georgia flu outbreak out in *Station Eleven*, his first trip is to the supermarket to stock up on as many trollies full of food as will fit in his car. Food is also key in Orwell's *Nineteen Eighty-Four*. Only the worst is available under the new regime: Winston's hallway smells of boiled cabbage, and the gin is synthetic and barely palatable. When he and Julia meet above the antique shop, she brings contraband with her – sugar, proper bread, jam, milk and real coffee. The food in dystopian fiction, so often found only in tins, is rarely this appetizing – it's necessary, but not desirable.

Happily, this bleak culinary landscape is not at all my experience of eating from tins. With the right ones in your cupboard – beans (baked and otherwise), various fish, tomatoes, coconut and condensed milks – you'll be able to rustle up something great without leaving the house. I appreciate their relaxed ease, the way that they sit quietly in the kitchen until I can make use of them, happily travelling with me from house to house, and finding a home on new shelves. I love the bright and jolly designs on my collection of sardine tins – ones that hail from Portugal, and Italy – offering some colour and light on a grey October day.

Perhaps it's the catastrophizer in me – the tendency I have to imagine all the worst possible outcomes – that means the apocalyptic stories have always had an enormous impact. Whatever happens, I feel reassured that I can visualize the weeks of meals we could subsist on if I needed to make sole use of my store cupboard. And, while we anticipate the coming apocalypse, my tins wait patiently, ready to help when I want something nice and easy for supper.

Ten bean chilli

I always have a stockpile of beans in the cupboard. I have tinned ones of different varieties to add to a soup or a stew, or to blitz to a smooth, calico-coloured purée. But I also like having the dried ones; ones that bounce satisfyingly as you pour them into a bowl, and need a day of soaking before they'll yield to a sauce. Serve this chilli with cornbread, some grated cheese, and plenty of sliced jalapeño peppers, if you're serving a crowd, or on toast for an easy supper.

Serves 6

1. Soak the beans overnight, or for a full day while you're at work. They'll take up quite a bit of water, so make sure they're covered with at least 1½ litres/6½ cups.

2. Once the beans have had their soaking time, put the dried chillies in a bowl, and pour the coffee over. Leave them to rehydrate for at least 20 minutes while you get on with everything else.

3. Warm the oil in a large saucepan, and fry the onion, carrot, and celery for about 10 minutes until soft. Add the garlic, and fry until fragrant.

4. Add the cumin, cayenne pepper, oregano, bay leaves, and cinnamon, and cook for about 5 minutes, until the vegetables are completely coated.

5. Take the chillies out of the coffee, and dice finely. Add the chillies and the coffee to the pot, and allow them to bubble away for a couple of minutes. Drain the beans, and tip these in along with the tinned tomatoes. Bring to the boil, then reduce to a simmer. Add the chipotle sauce, and the sugar, and season with salt and pepper.

6. Simmer gently, uncovered, for at least an hour, until the beans are tender and the sauce is thick and rich.

500g/3 cups dried beans*
15g/½oz dried ancho chillies
300ml/1¼ cups hot coffee
2tbsp groundnut oil
2 large brown onions, diced
1 large carrot, diced
2 stalks celery, diced
3 cloves garlic, minced
2tsp ground cumin
1tsp cayenne pepper
2tsp dried oregano
3 bay leaves
1tsp ground cinnamon
2 x 400g/14oz tin chopped tomatoes
2tbsp chipotle sauce
2tbsp dark brown sugar
Salt and black pepper

* I use a ten-bean mix, but use whatever you fancy – a mixture of a few types is good.

Sardine, chilli, and breadcrumb pasta

80g/2¾oz dried spaghetti

1 x 120g/4oz tin sardines in olive oil

3tbsp breadcrumbs

1 shallot, sliced

1 long red chilli, deseeded and finely sliced

1tbsp capers, rinsed and drained

½ lemon

When I was little, I only knew of tinned sardines from Enid Blyton novels, in which they were inexplicably squashed onto slices of ginger cake and eaten at midnight feasts. Now, I wouldn't be without them in my cupboard, and employ them frequently in this supper; the work of moments, and ideal for late arrivals home. There are weeks, either busy or lazy, when I end up eating it more than once.

Serves 1

1. Fill your biggest pot with water, and put it on to boil. I know it's just you, but even a single serving of pasta needs room to move. Season the water – it should be as salty as the sea. When the water has reached a rolling boil, add the spaghetti, and cook until al dente.

2. Meanwhile, open the tin of sardines. Pour half of the oil into a frying pan, and warm through. Add the breadcrumbs (they'll soak up all the oil), and stir until they are crunchy and golden. Tip into a bowl and set aside.

3. Tip the rest of the oil into the pan. Add the shallot, and cook until soft and translucent. Add the chilli, and stir.

4. Flake the sardines in the tin, and add them to the shallot and chilli. Stir through; keep a few fillets in larger chunks if you prefer. Stir in the capers.

5. Scoop out a mug of the pasta cooking water and set it aside. Drain the pasta, and then toss it into the pan of sardines. Add a splash of cooking water, and a squeeze of lemon juice, and stir over a low heat until combined.

6. Transfer to a bowl, and top with the breadcrumbs. Serve immediately.

Coffee ice

350ml/1½ cups freshly
brewed coffee
350g/1½ cups
condensed milk
350g/1½ cups
evaporated milk

I often feel like making ice cream late at night, to share
with whoever is in the house the next day. But, most
of the time, it requires a full fridge: double cream, egg
yolks, plenty of milk, and a good amount of stirring time
as you make a custard. One lazy Sunday, inspired by the
Vietnamese coffees on Broadway Market, my friend Nicola
and I whisked up a batch of this in moments, using what
was already in the cupboard. It has been a game changer.

Makes enough for 8

1. Whisk all the ingredients together in a container with
a good lid. Transfer to the freezer for an hour, and then
bring out and whisk vigorously to break up the ice crystals.

2. Repeat this every hour for the first few hours of freezing,
until the ice cream is nearly solid.

3. Bring the container out of the freezer about 10 minutes
before you'd like to serve it, and scoop it out with a hot
spoon.

Hallowe'en parties

There are many odd things to put down, and, lest who reads them
may fancy that I dined too well before I left Bistritz, let me put down
my dinner exactly. I dined on what they called 'robber steak' – bits of
bacon, onion, and beef, seasoned with red pepper, and strung on sticks,
and roasted over the fire, in the simple style of the London cat's meat!
Dracula, Bram Stoker

We didn't celebrate Hallowe'en when I was a child; trick-or-
treating wasn't the norm in our neighbourhood, and so knocking
on doors and asking for sweets was generally frowned upon. Our
experience, therefore, was a vicarious one – reading Goosebumps
books, watching Hallowe'en episodes of our favourite television
shows, and annual viewings of Bette Midler in *Hocus Pocus*. As
teenagers, my sister and I attended a handful of Hallowe'en parties,
but they were nothing like the one in Agatha Christie's novel – with
apple bobbing and games (and murder) – and more like the one in
Mean Girls, with everyone dressed in impossibly tiny outfits.

It wasn't until my job as a nanny that I really immersed myself
in preparations for Hallowe'en. For weeks beforehand, we spent
bus journeys home from school discussing costumes and routes
for collecting sweets. On the night itself, I stayed in the house,
a warming pot of curry on the stove, and a bowl of wrapped
chocolates on the table, ready to hand them out when the
doorbell rang. My charges arrived back pink-cheeked and with
bags full of sugar, and we sat with big bowls of the curry, making
plans for the costumes the next year. That night, I retreated to
bed with *The Woman in Black*, determined to scare myself silly.

Though I spent time running away from vampires and ghouls in
my childhood nightmares, it is domestic horror that more reliably
haunts me now. I can read Frankenstein and Dracula without
much loss of sleep, but am deeply affected by the creeping horror
of *The Haunting of Hill House* or *The Magic Toyshop* or *The Wasp
Factory*. I love these stories; love the chill that creeps down the
back of my neck and the way my heart races when I catch my
reflection in the mirror. They're ideal reading for the last weeks
of October, when the air is cold and crisp, ideal for snuggling up
under a blanket with a book.

Saag paneer and paratha

When the leaves start to turn

PARATHA
250g/1¾ cups + 2tbsp plain/all-purpose flour
½tsp salt
3tbsp melted ghee
250ml/1 cup lukewarm water

CURRY
250g/9oz paneer, cubed
2tbsp ghee (or groundnut oil)
2 brown onions, sliced
A generous pinch of salt
3 cloves garlic, crushed
2tsp garam masala
1tsp ground cumin
1tsp ground turmeric
1tsp chilli flakes
Black pepper
750g/1lb 10oz frozen spinach
2tbsp tomato paste
3tbsp natural yoghurt

This is perfect for the sort of Hallowe'en party I enjoy hosting. Make a giant pot of it (double or triple the amounts below – it's so easy to scale up), have some ghost stories at the ready, and eat generous bowlfuls by candlelight while you attempt to scare the rest of the group silly.

Serves 4

1. First, prepare the paratha dough. Pour the flour and salt into a bowl. In a jug, add 2 teaspoons of the melted ghee to the water, and then slowly pour into the flour, stirring to incorporate. Knead for 5–10 minutes, until the dough is soft and smooth, then return to the bowl, cover with a tea towel, and leave for 30 minutes while you make the curry.

2. Warm a dry pan over a moderate heat. Add the paneer, and brown all over. Remove and set aside.

3. Melt the ghee in a large saucepan and fry the onions, with the salt, for about 5 minutes, until they've started to soften. Add the garlic and cook for a couple of minutes, and then add the spices, chilli, and a good grinding of pepper. Cook for 5 minutes over a moderate heat, stirring frequently so they don't burn.

4. Add the frozen spinach, and stir as it defrosts. Stir in the tomato paste. Cook for 15 minutes, and then add the paneer. Turn off the heat, and add the yoghurt.

5. To shape the paratha, cut the dough into 8 pieces. Roll out into a thin circle, brush with the remaining melted ghee, and then fold in half. Brush with more ghee, and then fold in half again, so you have a triangle. Roll out carefully (or all the ghee will burst out) to lengthen, until the breads are a 2mm/¹⁄₁₆in thick. Lay in a hot, dry pan, and cook until the underside is covered with golden brown patches. Flip over and cook until the bread is flaky, cooked through, and has browned spots on both sides. Store the bread wrapped in a clean tea towel while you make the rest.

6. Warm the curry through, and serve the breads hot, with plenty of lime pickle alongside.

Robber steak

In Jonathan Harker's journal, kept as he travelled east to Transylvania at the urging of Count Dracula, he recalls stopping for a meal that reminds him of London street food. The dish he eats is robber steak, perfect for this time of year – the paprika and roasted peppers are both wonderfully warming on a cold October night.

Makes 2 generous skewers

1. First, roast the pepper. This can be done in advance, if that's easier; I often store a few in the fridge to have in pasta or sandwiches. Over an open flame on your hob, or in a hot oven, char the pepper until completely black. Place into a plastic bag and tie it closed. Leave until cool before rubbing off the charred skin.

2. Soak the skewers in a bowl of water for at least 15 minutes – this will prevent them catching fire. Cut the beef into generous chunks, and place in a bowl with the olive oil and paprika. Toss until completely covered.

3. Thread the bacon onto the skewer and weave it around pieces of beef, shallots and red pepper. Don't crowd the skewers too much, or the fat of the bacon won't cook properly.

4. Heat your griddle or barbeque until smoking hot, and place the skewers onto it. Cook until blackening in places, then turn the skewer. Continue cooking until the bacon fat has rendered and crisped up a little. Eat immediately.

1 long red/bell pepper
150g/5½oz beef (sirloin or fillet will be best here)
1tbsp olive oil
1tsp smoked paprika
4 rashers streaky bacon
3 small shallots, halved

EQUIPMENT
2 wooden skewers

When the leaves start to turn

Pistachio and chocolate cookies

125g/1¼ cups shelled pistachio nuts
75g/⅓ cup golden caster/superfine sugar
125g/½ cup butter
100g/½ cup light brown sugar
1 egg
1tsp vanilla paste
200g/1½ cups plain/all-purpose flour
1½tsp baking powder
150g/5½oz dark/bittersweet chocolate, chopped
A generous pinch of flaky sea salt

EQUIPMENT
Food processor

At the end of *The Wonderful Wizard of Oz*, Dorothy and her new friends are given four types of cookies and three types of cake to feast on. In honour of their battle with the Wicked Witch of the West, I'm suggesting these – filled with delightfully green pistachio nuts. A whole batch cooling on a rack is a welcome sight in the kitchen, but alternatively you can bake just a couple at a time, and eat them straight off the tray, your nose in a book, and the lights dimmed to deter any trick-or-treaters.

Makes 16

1. Blitz the pistachio nuts with a tablespoon of the golden caster sugar, until they form a thick paste.

2. Beat the pistachio paste and butter until soft, then add the remaining sugars. Continue beating until light and creamy, when the sugar no longer feels grainy between your fingers. Add the egg, and vanilla, and beat until combined. Fold in the flour, and baking powder, followed by the chocolate.

3. Split the dough into 16 pieces, and roll into balls. It will be quite sticky, but you want it to be. Place on a freezer-proof plate, ensuring the balls aren't touching, and place in the freezer for at least an hour, or overnight if that's easier.

4. Preheat the oven to 180C fan/400F/gas 6 and transfer the frozen biscuit dough onto lined baking sheets, giving them space to spread. Place in the oven for 15 minutes, until puffed and risen. They will be very soft. Sprinkle with flaky sea salt as soon as they come out of the oven. Cool on the sheet for 10 minutes, and then on a wire rack. The biscuits will collapse and harden as they cool, but will remain chewy in the middle.

Seasonal soups

Beautiful soup! Who cares for fish,
Game, or any other dish?
Who would not give all else for two
Pennyworth only of beautiful Soup?
Alice's Adventures in Wonderland, Lewis Carroll

There is little that comforts so effectively and efficiently as soup.
I always have tubs of it in the freezer, ready to be called upon on
evenings when I'm poorly, or snowed under. When I was sick on
the sofa in my mum's house, she'd head out and buy a chicken,
simmering it down slowly over an afternoon (the recipe for this
soup is in *The Little Library Cookbook*). When I moved to England,
the contents of the vegetable drawer often ended up in a big batch
of soup that would see me through the week. And after long weeks
of work in London, I'd arrive at the home of my Cotswolds family
on a late train, knowing there'd be a pot of butternut squash soup,
with chilli and peanut butter stirred through it, simmering on
the stove. When I need to be looked after, it is reassuring to know
that there is soup in my kitchen to play nursemaid, or provide a
welcome.

As a species we've been making soup for tens of thousands of
years. It is still found on tables throughout the world, a staple
that can be made with a glut of carrots, or the rarest mushroom.
In literature, soup speaks of warmth and of home. The English
prepare an enormous pot of thick soup for Billy Pilgrim and the
American prisoners in *Slaughterhouse Five*, a comfort in the midst
of horror. In *Pride and Prejudice*, Bingley orders a white soup to be
made when he wants to welcome Meryton society to Netherfield.
Tom brings endless bowls of chicken soup to Samuel in Steinbeck's
East of Eden. And Laurie Colwin notes that: 'to feel safe and warm
on a cold wet night, all you really need is soup'.

I make soup constantly in the autumn. Though I adore ice-cold
gazpacho in summer, and rich, umami noodle soups in the bleakest
winter months, the ones I make most often are vegetable soups
that sing of the season, made from whatever I can pick up on the
market. The addition of some spices and herbs, sharp cheese,
or the caramelization that comes from roasting, turns the most
humble of vegetables into a really special dish.

Roasted cauliflower and parsnip soup

SOUP

1 large head cauliflower, roughly chopped
3 parsnips, roughly chopped
Leaves from 8 sprigs thyme
2tbsp olive oil
1 medium brown onion, sliced
2 cloves garlic, crushed
1tsp smoked paprika
800ml/3½ cups vegetable stock
Salt and black pepper
2tbsp sour cream

TO SERVE

Thyme leaves
Sour cream
Croutons*

EQUIPMENT

Stab mixer or blender

* To make your own, coat chunks of day-old bread in a little olive oil and bake alongside the vegetables for 10 minutes

My pal Tom describes this soup as 'Christmas in a bowl'. He's not wrong – the parsnip is so distinctive, and screams of Christmas dinner, or of leftovers squashed into sandwiches on Boxing Day. I like parsnip too much to keep it for the festive season, and it works wonderfully here alongside the cauliflower.

Serves 4

1. Preheat the oven to 180C fan/400F/gas 6. Place the cauliflower and parsnips on a roasting tray. Sprinkle with the thyme leaves, and drizzle with 1 tablespoon of the olive oil. Roast for 30 minutes.

2. When the vegetables have been in the oven for about 15 minutes, warm the other tablespoon of oil in a saucepan, and add the onion. Stir for 10 minutes until soft and translucent, then add the garlic, and cook for a couple of minutes.

3. Tip the roasted cauliflower and parsnips into the saucepan, then add the paprika and stir. Pour the stock into the pan, and bring to a simmer. Cook for 5 minutes. Taste and season.

4. Turn off the heat, and allow the soup to cool. Blitz to a smooth purée in a blender or with a stab mixer. Warm over a medium heat, and then stir in the sour cream.

5. Serve hot with some more thyme, sour cream, and croutons.

Sort-of ribollita

I get through piles of kale when the weather is cool. When I was a nanny, I would roast big trays of it, seasoned with little more than olive oil and salt. The kids adored it. This soup combines that crunchy kale with a classic Italian soup – warming, filling, and full of hardy herbs.

Serves 6

1. Warm the oil in a large pan and fry the onion, celery, and carrot for 10 minutes until softened. Add the garlic, and the pancetta, if you're using it, and fry for a further 3 minutes.

2. Stir in the tomato paste, and then add the bay leaves, and rosemary, and season generously. Add the tomatoes.

3. Pour in the vegetable stock and bring to a gentle simmer. Add the cavolo nero, and cook at a gentle simmer for 90 minutes. Rinse the beans, and add them to the pot, then simmer for a final 20 minutes.

4. Meanwhile, roast the kale. Heat the oven to 200C fan/425F/gas 7. Spread the kale out on a baking sheet, and season with the oil and sea salt. Roast for 25 minutes, tossing once to ensure it is uniformly crisp.

5. Toast the sourdough, and rub with the crushed cloves of garlic. Place in the bottom of the bowls you'd like to serve in. Ladle the soup over the bread. Top with a handful of crispy kale. Serve with plenty of grated cheese, and pepper.

SOUP

2tbsp groundnut oil

2 brown onions, finely diced

2 stalks celery, finely diced

1 large carrot, finely diced

3 cloves garlic, minced

200g/1½ cups pancetta or lardons (optional)

1tbsp tomato paste

2 bay leaves

3 stalks rosemary, leaves finely chopped

Salt and black pepper

1 x 400g/14oz tin chopped tomatoes

2 litres/8½ cups vegetable stock

200g/5 cups cavolo nero, roughly chopped

2 x 400g tin/14oz cannellini beans, drained

TO SERVE

200g/5 cups kale, roughly chopped

3tbsp olive oil

1tsp flaky sea salt

6 slices sourdough

3 cloves garlic, crushed

Parmesan cheese (or a vegetarian alternative)

Spiced beetroot soup

2 large carrots
2 waxy potatoes
5 whole beetroot/beets
2 medium brown onions
A thumb-sized piece of ginger
1tbsp groundnut oil
1tsp mustard seeds
Salt and black pepper

TO SERVE
Crème fraîche/sour cream
Dill fronds

EQUIPMENT
Blender or stab mixer

The warmth of the mustard and ginger are a lovely accompaniment to the sweet earthiness of the beetroot here. It's also gloriously beautiful to look at; a rich purée in a bright purple-pink that would work just as well as a lipstick as it does in soup form. Find some rye bread to dip into it, and serve in generous portions in deep bowls.

Serves 6

1. Scrub the carrots, potatoes, and beetroot, and peel the onions and ginger. Dice the vegetables into roughly even pieces.

2. Warm the oil in a saucepan, and tip in the vegetables. Add the mustard seeds and seasoning. Cook for 5 minutes.

3. Add 600ml/2½ cups water, and bring to the boil. Reduce to a simmer and cook for 40 minutes, until the vegetables are soft. Remove from the heat, allow to cool a little, then blitz to a smooth purée in a blender or with a stab mixer.

4. Warm through (or chill completely – it works cold too), and serve with crème fraîche and dill.

When the leaves start to turn

More books for evenings when you feel a chill return to the air...

Swan about campus and take in a classics class in the company of Richard, Charles, Camilla, Henry, and Francis in *The Secret History* (just try not to bring up Bunny). Join Bilbo Baggins, *The Hobbit*, for an unexpected party in the Shire, and an adventure through Middle Earth. Head back to school with Erica Yurken, and commit some time to *Hating Alison Ashley*. Sip on a cocktail in the Oxfordshire dining room on the night before *The Shooting Party*. Lose yourself in books and words alongside William *Stoner*. Bake an enormous pumpkin pie with Ma Ingalls in the *Little House in the Big Woods*. Stumble over the cobbles in Edinburgh with the eponymous teacher and her handpicked group of girls in *The Prime of Miss Jean Brodie*. Run alongside the train with Bobbie in *The Railway Children*. Head off to Miss Cackle's Academy with *The Worst Witch*, Mildred Hubble. Avoid catching your reflection in the mirror after being thoroughly terrified by *The Woman in Black*. Enjoy a birthday cake, topped with initials spelled out in Smarties, with the heroine of *The Story of Tracy Beaker*. Hunt out a mysterious dog on the Devonshire moors with Dr Watson in *The Hound of the Baskervilles*. Take to the baseball diamond with the Westish team in *The Art of Fielding*. Join Marianne and Connell, a couple of *Normal People*, at university in Dublin. Find a carriage on the Hogwarts Express with Harry, Ron, and Hermione in *Harry Potter and the Prisoner of Azkaban*, but make sure you have some chocolate on hand to combat the Dementors.

As the days grow short

As the days grow short

*We feel cold, but we don't mind it, because we will not come to
harm. And if we wrapped up against the cold, we wouldn't feel
other things, like the bright tingle of the stars, or the music of the
Aurora, or best of all the silky feeling of moonlight on our skin.
It's worth being cold for that.*
Northern Lights, Philip Pullman

I always feel a frisson of excitement as December approaches. Those
final two months of the year – a whirlwind of Bonfire Night fireworks,
Christmas parties, lights being strung up around the town, far too
much mulled wine, and long sessions of wrapping with brown paper
and string – are my favourite of the year. I love having a reason to
find the perfect book for a friend, or to spend long hours filling a line
of bottles and jars with edible gifts. Despite the creeping cold, the
end of the year seems to bring with it unmistakable warmth, a joyful
anticipation of the season to come.

It is not just the promise of Christmas and the New Year that
fills me with joy. Even in Australia, when I was young, the first months
of winter were the ones I looked forward to all year. They did not
lead to Christmas, of course, but they invited time for curling up with
books, for warming socks over the heater, for an extra blanket on our
beds. The houses in Queensland are not built for the cold and so,
despite the relatively tropical climate, we hopped on tip-toe across the
icy tiled floors, and came down to breakfast each morning wrapped
tightly in our warmest dressing gowns. We made stews, and ate plenty
of hot buttered toast for tea, and cooked dishes we wouldn't have
dreamed of in the oppressive heat of summer: pastries, pies, and all
manner of puddings.

During my first winter in England, I was a theatre intern wrapped
in gloves and a scarf, tapping away at an ancient PC in an unheated
room above a pub. My time in this particular theatre was brief, but it
was formative – I saw my first snow, learnt more about the industry
than I could have imagined, and sat propped up at the bar after
closing, drinking wine and whisky with new pals. I also remember

this time as being one of voracious reading; all those books with winter
and snow and Christmas contained within them suddenly made sense,
and I reread all my childhood favourites: *A Christmas Carol, Little
Women, The Lion, the Witch and the Wardrobe*, and Agatha Christie's
The Adventure of the Christmas Pudding. They're stories I still
continue to return to, year after year, once the warmest duvet comes
out of storage and goes back onto my bed.

Quiet evenings in

...an exquisite scent of olives and oil and juice rose from the great brown dish as Marthe, with a little flourish, took the cover off. The cook had spent three days over that dish. And she must take great care, Mrs Ramsay thought, diving into the soft mass to choose a specially tender piece for William Bankes. And she peered into the dish, with its shiny walls and its confusion of savoury brown and yellow meats, and its bay leaves and its wine...
To the Lighthouse, Virginia Woolf

Though I approach the festive season every year hoping to catch up with a long list of friends, scheduling film screenings, and shopping trips, and endless Sunday afternoons in the pub, I'm aware of my own inability to maintain this sort of social calendar. I find myself longing for a day in by myself, fearing burnout if I don't allocate time to recharge. When I do decide to embrace some time alone, I turn (as ever) to books, and to food. I want to fill the house with the scent of something delicious, and devote hours to a dish that demands my time, though not my attention – allowing plenty of opportunities for sitting on the sofa with a book.

In the colder months, I am rarely deterred by a lengthy cooking time. I know and appreciate the joy of a quick supper, but there is something reassuring about a dish you just can't rush: meat that needs time to become meltingly tender; sauces that plip away slowly, reducing and thickening over the course of an afternoon; or an ice cream that requires the freezer overnight. The longer a dish takes, the more time I know I have for curling up and reading. It seems like the perfect deal.

For the most part, the steps in the recipes that follow here are simple, and you can then leave the pot to work its magic. Spend the time that this affords you with diverting stories: a day with Miss Pettigrew, a journey down the Thames with three men in a boat, a trip to the Isle of Skye with Woolf's Ramsays. Though I'll eventually invite people round to share in the culinary spoils, these are dishes that can be kept and warmed through again, so that first evening with them is one you can enjoy alone.

Lamb stew

On a cold night on the Thames, *Three Men in a Boat* prepared an entirely inauthentic Irish stew. Alongside the meat, the potatoes, the cabbage, and the peas, they throw in half a pork pie, boiled bacon, potted salmon, and a few eggs. I wouldn't suggest that it's a vehicle for quite that much, but on a slow, cosy night in, it's such a wonderful way to, as the men put it, get 'rid of such a lot of things'.

Serves 6

1. Roughly chop one of the onions, one of the carrots, and the stalks of celery. Put the scrag end in a large lidded saucepan with the chopped vegetables. Cover with 2 litres/8½ cups of water, and add the peppercorns. Bring to a simmer, and then cook with the lid on for 2 hours, until the meat is falling off the bone.

2. Strain the stock, discard the vegetables, and pull the meat from the bones. Discard the bones and set the meat to one side.

3. Chop the rest of the vegetables: the onions into slices and the carrots into thick coins. Warm the oil in the pan and fry the onion and carrot for 10 minutes until softened. Pour in the stock, and then add the potatoes. Simmer very gently (do not let it boil) for 45 minutes with the lid on. Add the shredded cabbage, and the lamb. Taste the stock and season with salt and pepper. Simmer, covered, for another half-hour.

4. Five minutes before you plan to serve, add the frozen peas and parsley. Serve hot, in big bowls, beside a crackling fire. Leave the cold-weather boating to someone else.

4 brown onions
4 large carrots
2 stalks celery
1kg/2lb 4oz scrag end of lamb
10 whole black peppercorns
2tbsp groundnut oil
400g/14oz Charlotte potatoes (or any other floury variety), peeled and chopped into chunks
1 small white cabbage, shredded
Salt and black pepper
150g/1¼ cups frozen peas
A handful of chopped parsley

Boeuf en daube à la Provençale

In *To the Lighthouse*, the Ramsays' cook spends days preparing a boeuf en daube, a dish worthy of the flourish it is presented with. The recipe varies from region to region, but the presence of olives in Woolf's description suggests it hails from Provence, so the dish below is adapted from Julia Child's '*à la Provençale*' version. It takes long hours, but is, I assure you, entirely worth your time.

Serves 8–10

1. Place the beef in a large bowl, with the thyme, bay leaves, 2 crushed cloves of the garlic, onions, carrots, salt, pepper, and wine. Stir, cover and leave for 6 hours to marinate.

2. Fry the bacon in a frying pan until cooked but not crispy. Spread the flour onto a plate. Pull the beef out of the marinade, draining over the bowl before tossing it in the flour. Shake off any excess and set aside.

3. Preheat the oven to 150C fan/325F/gas 3. In a casserole dish, layer up the ingredients. Start with a third of the bacon, then half the mushrooms and a tin of tomatoes. Put a third of the floured beef on top, then a third of the vegetables from the marinade. Repeat with the same layers and finish with the final layer of beef, the last of the vegetables and the bacon. Pour the marinade into the pot. You want the liquid to just cover the ingredients, so add some beef stock if needed. Cover and cook for 3 hours.

4. Check it after a couple of hours, removing the lid if the liquid looks a little thin. Just before the stew comes out, blitz or finely chop the anchovies, capers and remaining garlic cloves, then mix with the oil from the anchovy tin, the olive oil, and red wine vinegar. Stir this mixture and the olives into the stew and return to the oven for 2 hours.

5. Take the pot out of the oven and allow to cool. Place it in the fridge for 24 hours. This isn't compulsory, but the flavour really does improve if you leave it overnight. When you're ready to eat, reheat it at 150C/325F/gas 3 for an hour. Sprinkle with parsley and serve.

1.5kg/3lb 5oz shin beef (or another stewing cut), cut into large chunks
1tsp thyme leaves
3 bay leaves
4 cloves garlic
4 brown onions, sliced
3 carrots, sliced
2tsp flaky sea salt
Black pepper
600ml/2½ cups red wine (a full-bodied French red is ideal)
250g/9oz unsmoked back bacon, chopped
120g/scant 1 cup plain/all-purpose flour
150g/2½ cups chestnut/cremini mushrooms, finely sliced
2 x 400g/14oz tin chopped tomatoes
Beef stock (if you need more liquid)
1 x 50g/1¾oz tin anchovy fillets in oil
2tbsp capers
2tbsp olive oil
3tbsp red wine vinegar
250g/2½ cups pitted black olives
A handful of parsley leaves

An ambrosial dessert

ICE CREAM
150g/½ cup honey
400ml/1¾ cups double/
heavy cream
200ml/generous ¾ cup
milk
1 vanilla pod/bean
A pinch of salt
6 egg yolks

FIGS
8 figs
2tsp runny honey

PRALINE
40g/⅓ cup whole
almonds
70g/⅓ cup caster/
superfine sugar
1tbsp cold water
Juice of ½ lemon

CREAM
100ml/scant ½ cup
double/heavy cream
½tsp vanilla bean paste

Miss Pettigrew Lives for a Day is a joy of a book: a story about uninspired, down-at-heel governess Guinevere Pettigrew. After an extraordinary day, and through a series of entirely unexpected events, she finds herself enjoying an 'ambrosial dessert', at a fancy party in the early hours of the morning. Her enjoyment of the dessert, and of the situation she suddenly finds herself in, is palpable, and stayed with me long after I finished reading. Ambrosial suggests figs and honey to me, so I have turned to them here.

Serves 4

1. Make the ice cream the day before you plan to eat. Bring the honey to a simmer in a small saucepan, and cook to a rich, dark amber. Put the pan in a bowl of cold water to stop it cooking.

2. While the honey is still warm and runny, add the cream and milk. Split the vanilla pod and add it too, along with a pinch of salt. Heat until almost simmering. Whisk the egg yolks in a separate bowl.

3. Pour the hot milk and cream over the yolks, whisking constantly. Wash out the saucepan, pour the custard back into it and place over a low heat. Stir with a wooden spoon until thick enough to coat the back of it. Remove the vanilla pod. Pour into a freezer-proof container, cover, and place in the fridge to cool completely.

4. Once cold, transfer to the freezer or to an ice-cream maker. If in the freezer, whisk vigorously every hour for the first 3 hours to break up any ice crystals, then leave to freeze for a few hours, or overnight.

5. To prepare the figs, heat the oven to 180C fan/400F/gas 6. Cut a cross almost completely through each fig. Stand them cut-side up in an ovenproof dish, drizzle over the honey and roast for 25 minutes, until soft and sticky.

6. To make the praline, place the almonds in the oven (while the figs are roasting) for 10 minutes, until fragrant

and slightly browned. Chop, then scatter in a single layer
onto a lined baking sheet. Place the sugar and water in a
pan, bring to the boil and then simmer until you have a rich
amber caramel. Add the lemon juice, then pour the liquid
over the almonds. Leave to cool and hardened, then chop
into shards.

7. To serve, whip the cream to soft peaks and fold in the
vanilla. Serve a scoop of the ice cream with a couple of
warm figs, a drizzle of their ambrosial liquor, a spoonful of
the cream and some praline.

The joy of toast

My hour for tea is half-past five, and my buttered toast waits for nobody.
The Woman in White, Wilkie Collins

When the days grow dark by four, and frost creeps across the windows in the kitchen, my thoughts turn to toast. When I was a nanny, my boss and I spent long hours sipping scalding hot mugs of tea, and piling everything we could find onto thick slices of toast. We went through jars of marmalade so numerous I could barely keep up with demand, and spread butter thickly onto each small crust left on our plates. Nowadays, more frequently than I like to admit, my housemate will whip up his 'Tom Jacob special': a slice of toast spread with butter, Marmite, and peanut butter, and then topped with (stay with me) sauerkraut and Tabasco sauce. We'll make a pot of tea, and take a small break from our work. It is indecently good. It's also perhaps evidence that you could put pretty much anything on toast and I'd wax lyrical about it.

Toast crops up so frequently in English stories that it has become a shorthand for familiarity and safety: Gandalf eats 'two whole loaves (with masses of butter…)' for breakfast in *The Hobbit*; Alice is reassured when she tastes hot buttered toast in the potion labeled 'Drink Me'; and Mary Poppins smells of white linen and toast. Sara and Becky toast muffins over the attic fire in *A Little Princess*, and the Baudelaire orphans remember burning toast when making breakfast for their parents in the first of Lemony Snicket's *A Series of Unfortunate Events*. The daily reliability of buttered toast in *The Woman in White* seems entirely natural; I can't imagine any other food being enjoyed with such regularity.

There is nothing that comforts and reassures quite like toast. Though his strident conservatism and anthropomorphic animals don't do much for me, Kenneth Grahame (and, through him, Toad) truly understood the glory of toast, spread thickly with butter. His words in *The Wind in the Willows* have stayed with me since I first read them, close to twenty-five years ago: buttered toast speaks of 'warm kitchens, of breakfasts on bright frosty mornings, of cosy parlour firesides on winter evenings, when one's ramble was over and slippered feet were propped on the fender…'

Apple, apple jelly, Parmesan and pepper

I make so much apple jelly every autumn that I am, inevitably, still eating it at Christmas. This is a great way to finish it up – on toast, with apple sliced as thinly as a sheet of paper, and some sharp, salty Parmesan cheese.

Serves 1

1. Toast the rye bread, spread with butter, and then apple jelly.

2. Slice the apple as thinly as you can, through the core. A mandoline is helpful, if you have one, or just use a very sharp knife. Remove any pips.

3. Layer the apple slices on top of the jelly, and top with Parmesan and a generous grinding of black pepper.

2 slices rye bread
Butter, for spreading
2tsp cider apple jelly (see p. 216)
½ crisp, eating apple
A small handful of Parmesan shavings (or a vegetarian alternative)
Black pepper

Marsala, mushrooms, and thyme

With the application of Marsala, and a little time (and thyme too), these mushrooms find themselves frequently on my table for breakfast, or for supper.

Serves 1

1. Melt the butter in a large frying pan and add the oil. Fry the shallot until softened, then add the garlic and fry until fragrant.

2. Tip in the mushrooms and cook over a moderate heat until golden around the edges, stirring occasionally. Add the thyme leaves.

3. Pour in the Marsala, and allow it to bubble away. Stir through the sour cream, then turn off the heat and season. Toast the bread, spread with butter, and spoon the mushrooms on top.

1tbsp butter
1tsp groundnut oil
1 banana shallot, sliced
1 garlic clove, minced
150g/2½ cups chestnut/cremini mushrooms, sliced
Leaves from 6 sprigs of thyme
2tbsp Marsala
1tbsp sour cream
Salt and black pepper
1 slice sourdough
Butter, for spreading

Sprouting broccoli, anchovy, boiled egg

1 egg
1 x 50g/1¾oz tin anchovy fillets in oil
2 cloves garlic, sliced
4 stalks sprouting broccoli
1 slice sourdough
Butter, for spreading
Black pepper

I am never without a tin of anchovies in the cupboard. Most often, they'll be employed in a pasta sauce, or squashed straight onto buttered toast late at night. Their intense flavour is one I took a little time to come round to, but it's now one that sways me each time I consider it: on a menu, or when I'm searching through my cupboards for inspiration. This version of eggs on toast was born of the latter.

Serves 1

1. Put a small pan of water on to boil. Once it is at a rolling boil, reduce to a simmer, so that the egg doesn't bounce about too much and crack. Lower in the egg on a spoon, and set a timer for 5 mins 30 seconds.

2. Pour the oil from the tin of anchovies into a frying pan. Once hot, add the anchovies and squash them into the oil. Add the garlic, and then the broccoli (if it's woody, chop the ends off). Fry over a moderate heat until the broccoli is crisp and browned in places.

3. Toast your sourdough and, once the timer pings, rinse the egg under lots of cold water. Crack the shell all over, peel it off carefully, and slice the egg in half.

4. Serve the toast, buttered, topped with the broccoli, egg, and a generous grinding of black pepper.

Bloody Mary guacamole, fried eggs, coriander

The cliché of a thirty-something sort-of Australian offering a recipe for avocado on toast is not lost on me. Avocado toast is ubiquitous where I grew up; even my stepdad Geoff, who likes toasted sandwiches filled with tinned spaghetti, has 'smashed avo' on his toast for breakfast. Here in England, the avocados I can lay my hands on are sometimes a little hit and miss – but if I happen upon a disappointing one, I have taken to making this guacamole with it, rather than slicing my avocado straight onto toast.

½ avocado
Juice from ½ lime
½tsp Worcestershire sauce
A couple of shakes of the Tabasco bottle
A pinch of celery salt
Black pepper
A slice from a grainy loaf of bread
1tsp groundnut oil
1 egg
A few coriander/cilantro leaves

Serves 1

1. Scoop the avocado out of its shell, and then mash with a fork. Add the lime juice, Worcestershire sauce, Tabasco, celery salt, and pepper. Give it a taste; you might fancy it a little spicier, or saltier, or sharper.

2. Toast the bread. Warm the oil in a small frying pan and, once it is smoking, crack in the egg. It will sputter and spit, so stand back a little. Once the white has become opaque, turn off the heat.

3. Spread the avocado over the toast, and top with the egg and some fresh coriander leaves. Serve immediately.

Cocktail parties

The longest and most destructive party ever held is now into its fourth generation, and still no one shows any signs of leaving. Somebody did once look at his watch, but that was eleven years ago, and there has been no follow-up.
Life, the Universe and Everything, Douglas Adams

I lived at home throughout university, and so the parties we had didn't generally happen at my house. They were also nothing like the 'grown-up' parties I had spent my childhood waiting and planning for; we didn't make canapés, or drink glasses of fizzy wine. Instead, we poured our bottles of cheap wine and spirits into buckets, and ladled the resulting (appalling) cocktail into plastic cups. We embraced any excuse for a costume party, and played endless drinking games. We had the raucous down, but the Gatsby-esque glamour I'd long lusted after was elusive.

In my London flat, I never had quite enough space to host proper parties. My bedroom was in the living room, and although I could get away with inviting everyone back for late-night croque monsieurs, or big bowls of pasta, starting the party there with any more than a handful of people always felt cramped. I also started to recognize that, as much as I wanted to play the hostess, crowded, boisterous parties left me cold; I hunted out corners to hide in, and good friends to pull away from the crowd. I realized that I enjoyed the preparation and the satisfaction of seeing a room full of people far more than the event itself. It's the making of lists and planning of menus I relish; I am always happiest at a party with an apron over my dress, or a tray of food in my hand.

In all honesty, I'm usually overwhelmed by the extravagance and decadence of Jay Gatsby's frequent parties, the dancing and cocktails at the soirée Margot Metroland hosts in *Vile Bodies*, or the idea of being passed over by Mr Darcy at a ball. But at Christmas, everything changes, and these fictional parties provide inspiration. I come out of my shell, and there's a crowd of people I want to catch up with, ham to be stuffed into rolls, canapés to be plated up (to soak up the drinks), carols to be sung and cocktails to be served. It's the one time of year when I aim to host a party Mr Fezziwig – he of the glorious annual party in *A Christmas Carol* – would be proud of.

Ginger beer ham on brioche buns

BRIOCHE BUNS

150ml/⅔ cup milk

150ml/⅔ cup water

25g/2tbsp fresh yeast
or 7g/1½tsp easy-action
yeast

2tbsp caster/superfine
sugar

1 egg

250g/1¾ cups + 2tbsp
plain/all-purpose flour

250g/1¾ cups strong
bread flour

50g/3½tbsp butter,
softened

A pinch of salt

1 egg, beaten

30g/¼ cup sesame
seeds

HAM

2 onions

1.2kg/2lb 10oz rolled
pork shoulder

1¼ litres/5½ cups
ginger beer

2tbsp seeded mustard

2tbsp golden syrup

TO SERVE

50g/3½tbsp butter

50g/2½tbsp chilli jam/
jelly

Jay Gatsby's Saturday extravaganzas are perhaps best remembered for the cocktails, the dancing, and their thinly disguised purpose: to attract Daisy Buchanan across the water to West Egg. But it would be remiss not to mention the food: 'spiced baked hams crowded against salads of harlequin design and pastry pigs and turkeys bewitched to a dark gold.' This ham is an adaptation of Nigella's famed Coca-Cola one, and is what I make at Christmas.

Makes 24 little rolls

1. First, make the brioche rolls. Warm the milk and water in a pan over the stove. When they're at room temperature, whisk in the yeast. Add the sugar, and the egg.

2. Combine the flours and salt in a bowl, and pour in the wet ingredients. Bring it together with your hands, and knead the dough by hand or in a mixer until smooth, elastic, and no longer sticky. Knead in the butter, a small piece at a time. Put the dough in a clean bowl, cover, and leave to double in size; it should take an hour or two, depending on how cold your kitchen is.

3. While the dough is rising, start on the ham. Peel the onions, slice them in half, and place in a large saucepan along with the ham. Pour over the ginger beer and bring to the boil over a moderate heat. Reduce to a gentle simmer, and cover the pan with foil or a lid so that the liquid doesn't boil off. Simmer for an hour and a half.

4. Once the dough has risen, weigh it, and divide it into 24 evenly sized pieces. Shape each into a ball, folding the dough underneath, and then rolling it on the work surface. Place the buns on a baking sheet lined with parchment paper, spacing them 2cm/ ¾in apart. Cover the sheets with a tea towel and allow the buns to rise again; they should bounce back when you prod them, and will have increased a little in size, though not as dramatically as the first rise.

5. Heat the oven to 200C fan/425F/gas 7. Paint the buns with the beaten egg, then sprinkle with sesame seeds. Bake for 15 minutes, until risen, and golden brown.

6. Turn the oven up to 220C fan/475F/gas 9. Take the ham out of the ginger beer, and snip away any string holding it together. Score a deep crosshatch into the fat, and place the ham in a small tray or wrap the base with foil, so there is as little space as possible for the golden syrup to escape and burn. Whisk together the mustard and golden syrup, and spoon it over the ham. Roast in the oven for 15–20 minutes. Do keep an eye on it, as the syrup can burn quickly at this temperature.

7. Leave the ham to cool a little, and then slice thinly. Split open the buns, spread with a little butter and chilli jam, and stuff with the ham. Serve warm or cold.

Crab cakes

CRAB CAKES

300g/10oz Maris Piper potatoes
300g/10oz tinned white crabmeat
2 spring onions/ scallions, finely sliced
Zest of 1 lemon
2 eggs
10g/½ cup chopped dill
15g/¾ cup chopped tarragon
20g/1 cup chopped parsley
3tbsp capers, chopped
Salt and black pepper

TO COOK

50g/heaped ⅓ cup plain/all-purpose flour
2 eggs, beaten
125g/1½ cups dried breadcrumbs
150ml/⅔ cup groundnut or vegetable oil

TO SERVE

1 lemon
Flaky sea salt
Mayonnaise and/or chilli sauce

If your budget can stretch to it, then do feel free to use fresh crabmeat in these. I'm much more likely to use tinned here (do try to look for ones that have been caught sustainably), keeping fresh crabmeat for eating on its own, tossed through pasta, or with a slice of buttered white bread. You can also make these into much larger patties, with other tinned fish (tuna works well), for supper.

Makes 30 little fish cakes

1. Peel and chop the potatoes into chunks. Place in a pot, cover with cold water, and bring to the boil. Simmer for 15 minutes, until soft. Drain, then press through a potato ricer, or mash in a bowl.

2. Mix the crabmeat, spring onions, and lemon zest through the potato. Crack the eggs and beat with a fork, then mix them in too. Add the chopped herbs and capers, and season.

3. Form into small balls, around the size of a walnut in its shell. Flatten a little, and place on a baking sheet. Put the sheet in the freezer for 15 minutes, or in the fridge for an hour if that's easier.

4. Set up a little production line to cook the crab cakes. Prepare a bowl with the flour, another with the beaten eggs, and a third with the breadcrumbs. Cover the crab cakes in flour, dip them in the egg, and then dredge in breadcrumbs. Place on a second baking sheet until you've prepped the whole batch.

5. Warm the oil in a frying pan over a moderate heat and, once hot, carefully place the crab cakes into it. Once they're golden brown underneath, flip them over, and allow to cook on the other side. Drain on some paper towels, and then give them a little squeeze of lemon and a few flakes of sea salt on top. Serve warm, with mayonnaise or chilli sauce, for dipping.

Porcini mushroom arancini

It's possible that I have made in excess of 1,000 of these arancini. In fact, that number feels like a somewhat conservative estimate; they're enormously popular as canapés at the weddings my friend Liv and I cater for, and we're always making them in enormous batches. I've yet to tire of them, as they offer everything I want from a canapé: they're salty, perfect with wine, easy to pick up, and incredibly moreish.

Makes 24 small arancini

1. Rehydrate the porcini mushrooms by covering them with boiling water. Leave for 20 minutes, then drain and chop, reserving the water.

2. Heat a thin layer of oil with a little butter in large pan. Cook the onions until translucent, then add the garlic and cook for a few minutes.

3. Add the rice and stir through the onions. Pour in the porcini mushroom liquid and stir as it bubbles away, then start adding the stock, a ladleful at a time. After about 10 minutes, add the chopped fresh and porcini mushrooms. Keep adding stock until the rice is cooked through, with no chalky interior. Taste, and season with salt and pepper. Allow to cool, fold in the mozzarella, and then refrigerate until cold.

4. Roll the chilled risotto into ping-pong-sized balls. Set up an assembly line. Dip each arancini first into the flour, then into the beaten egg, then into the panko breadcrumbs.

5. Heat the vegetable oil in a large, deep pan to 180C/355F. Cook the arancini in small batches, submerging them in the oil until golden. Drain on paper towels, and sprinkle with flaky sea salt before serving. I love them alongside a sauce made from chopped capers, shallots, parsley, and a little red wine vinegar, or some of the pesto from p. 179.

ARANCINI
10g/⅓ cup dried porcini mushroom
1tbsp oil
1tbsp butter
2 brown onions, diced
4 cloves garlic, finely chopped
300g/scant 1½ cups arborio rice
Up to 800ml/3½ cups mushroom or vegetable stock
125g/2 cups chestnut/cremini mushrooms, finely diced
2 balls Mozzarella, diced
Salt and black pepper

FOR COOKING
50g/⅓ cup flour
1 egg
80g/2 cups panko breadcrumbs
2 litres/8¾ cups vegetable oil

Bronx cocktail

50ml/3½ tbsp orange juice
100ml/scant ½ cup gin
20ml/1½tbsp sweet vermouth
20ml/1½tbsp dry vermouth
A handful of ice cubes

Each Friday, before Jay Gatsby's weekend parties, crates of oranges and lemons were delivered to his door. On Mondays, the squeezed-out orange halves were collected, stacked back up in the crates. His bartenders had clearly spent the Saturday making these, one of the five drinks named for the New York boroughs; the Manhattan is the most famous now, but at one point four of the cocktails were relatively well known (not so much the Staten Island). Popular during prohibition, possibly because it helped disguise the taste of the less-than-perfect gin available, the Bronx cocktail is a martini with fresh, zingy orange: a perfect Christmas party drink.

Makes 2

1. Tip all ingredients into a cocktail shaker, and shake vigorously for a couple of seconds.

2. Strain into 2 cocktail glasses and serve immediately.

Seasonal gifts

Perhaps because they had been working so hard, Christmas day seemed the loveliest they had known. Nothing was very different from other Christmases; but somehow it seemed a particularly gay day. Their stockings bulged when they woke, and besides all the usual things in them, there were large white sugar pigs with pink noses and wool tails.
Ballet Shoes, Noel Streatfeild

I had been in London for nearly two years when I moved to Hackney. A friend and I rented a tiny flat, with walls painted a dull shade of magnolia, and with a miniature, windowless bathroom. We moved in November, just as the trees had dropped the last of their leaves, and walked in circles around London Fields, kicking our way through the piles that lay beneath the trees. I had just started my first proper paid job in theatre, and London was starting to feel like a proper home.

As I began to make plans for Christmas, I felt the financial impact of paying a sizeable deposit, and of moving into an unfurnished flat. And so, while walking along Ridley Road Market on the way to work, I decided that all my gifts that year would need to be edible ones. I was cash-poor, but time-rich, and I had a glorious new kitchen to work in. The next few weeks were a flurry of cordials, marmalades, chutneys, pickles, and jams. I bought fruit and vegetables priced at £1 a bowl, turned them into preserves, spooned my wares into jars I'd collected (thanks to my mum's example, I'd long kept a box of rinsed-out jars in the hall cupboard), and tied ribbons around them. A week before Christmas, as I boxed them all up so I could take them to the Cotswolds, snow began to fall thickly outside.

Even when my December has been filled with work and events, I've continued my annual gift-making tradition. I still keep a box of jars, ready for December, in the hall cupboard. I'm constantly thinking of new recipes that might work nicely in jars, boxes, or bottles under the tree. I find inspiration in the ingredients that are piled up in the markets, and in those dream Christmases I read about in books as a child, when I longed for snow, and stockings that hung over a fireplace, filled with edible treats.

Apple, pear, and chilli chutney

When there are piles of apples and pears in the markets, towards the end of autumn, it feels like a prompt from nature to make this edible Christmas gift. This chutney will hang about in the cupboard until the spring if the recipient prefers, but I am wont to encourage them to open it up in the days following Christmas, so it can be spooned liberally onto crackers and good cheese. The chutney steals its method from Teresa's date and apple chutney, which I read about in Diana Henry's *Salt, Sugar, Smoke*: chop your ingredients into small dice and cook them for an hour before you add the vinegar and sugar.

1kg/2lb 4oz eating apples, peeled, cored and finely diced

500g/1lb 2oz pears, peeled and finely diced

500g/1lb 2oz onions, peeled and finely diced

500g/2½ cups granulated sugar

300ml/1¼ cups cider vinegar

1tsp salt

1tsp chilli flakes

Makes 4 x 300ml/10oz jars

1. Place the fruit and onions in a large saucepan, and cook over a low heat for an hour, stirring regularly so they don't stick. The apples will give off plenty of liquid, so you don't need to add any at this stage.

2. After an hour, stir in the sugar, vinegar, salt, and chilli. Bring to a simmer and reduce until thickened, stirring regularly. To check if it is done, draw a line along the bottom of the pan; when the chutney is ready, the line won't flood with liquid.

3. Spoon into sterilized jars (see p. 158). They will keep in a cool, dark place for at least 6 months, but have yet to last this long in my house.

Almond and pistachio biscotti

100g/¾ cup almonds
50g/½ cup shelled pistachios
300g/2¼ cups plain/all-purpose flour
200g/1 cup caster/superfine sugar
1tsp baking powder
1tsp salt
2–3 eggs
Zest of 2 clementines
1tbsp fennel seeds
50g/⅓ cup icing/confectioner's sugar

These are brilliant biscuits to give away as gifts; they last longer than most baked goods, and are great to have around the house during the Christmas season, to pull out at a moment's notice when people drop round for a coffee. They were borne out of a deep affection for the nuts and biscuits left out on Christmas Eve for the birds and squirrels in L. M. Boston's *The Children of Green Knowe*. Fennel and clementine feel appropriately Christmassy, but you can replace them with other spices, or leave them plain.

Makes 24

1. Preheat the oven to 200C fan/425F/gas 7. Toast the almonds and pistachios in a dry pan. Don't let them colour too much; you want them to take on a little gold.

2. Mix the flour, sugar, baking powder, and salt together in a large bowl. Beat 2 of the eggs with the clementine zest, and pour this in, mixing with a wooden spoon. Knead the dough, adding some of the third egg if it is too dry; the dough should be workable, and not too sticky. Fold in the nuts and fennel seeds, ensuring they're evenly distributed.

3. Divide the dough into 2 logs, and place on a baking sheet, at least 5cm/2in apart. They'll be too wet to stay in a cylinder in the oven, so don't worry when they start to spread out. Dust the tops with a layer of icing sugar. Transfer to the oven for 25 minutes.

4. Once the logs of dough are firm, and cooked inside (a skewer will come out clean), remove from the oven, and reduce the heat to 160C fan/350F/gas 4.

5. Allow them to cool only a little, until you can touch them, and then slice into finger-width pieces. Lay them out on a lined baking sheet, cut-side up. Bake for 15 minutes, then turn them over and give them a final 15 minutes. They should be crisp; perfect for dipping into coffee.

Cranberry cordial

1kg/2lb 4oz fresh or
frozen cranberries
1 litre/4¼ cups water
500g/2 cups caster/
superfine sugar
3 cinnamon sticks
Strips of zest and juice
from 5 lemons

EQUIPMENT
A piece of muslin/
cheesecloth

I make pints of this every Christmas, and drink it as much
as possible in the final weeks of the year. It's a deep,
rich, pink-red, and looks lush in bottles underneath the
Christmas tree. Drink it with fizzy wine, with sparkling
water, or have just a dash of it with gin over ice.

Makes about 1 litre/4¼ cups

1. Pour the cranberries and the water into a saucepan.
Find a comfortable seat somewhere, and pop the
cranberries between your fingers. Don't worry if you miss
some, but popping them open before you start will ensure
your cordial is as strong and delicious as possible.

2. Bring to the boil over a moderate heat, then tip in
the sugar and cinnamon sticks, and simmer gently for
15 minutes.

3. Add the strips of lemon zest and juice, and simmer for
a further 5 minutes.

4. Turn off the heat, and allow the cordial to sit and cool
for 10 minutes. Strain through a clean piece of muslin, and
pour into sterilized bottles (see p. 158).

Scandinavian Christmas Eve

That morning Pippi was busy making pepparkakor – a kind of
Swedish cookie. She had made an enormous amount of dough and
rolled it out on the kitchen floor. 'Because,' said Pippi to her little
monkey, 'what earthly use is a baking board when one plans to
make at least five hundred cookies?'
Pippi Longstocking, Astrid Lindgren (translated by Edna Hurup)

In my early twenties, I moved ten thousand miles away from home in search of something I couldn't quite define – independence, adventure, a hope that I could fall in love with a city. To my eternal pleasure (and relief) I found all of this. A decade on, it is England I call home. My first year was hard, and often lonely. I missed my family desperately, and was quietly dreading the thought of Christmas without them. But when December arrived that year, heralded by a small flurry of snow, there was something about it that felt undeniably right.

The very nature of Christmas, so richly steeped in ritual, means that it serves to remind us of things that are different from years that have gone before. Of people who are no longer seated around the table: of fallings-out, of break-ups, of those who have died. The arrival of the season is inescapable, and so we have no choice but to adapt, making up new rituals, or embracing the old ones as best we can.

On the other side of the world, my family's holiday season continues without me. My separation from them is eased by the fact that, early on, I was adopted into another family: half-English, half-Swedish. Through them I have been introduced to an entirely different way of doing Christmas: the Swedish smörgåsbord on Christmas Eve, stockings (or Wellington boots) that hang heavily from the hearth, the construction of a gingerbread house, a long Boxing Day walk, truly dreadful Christmas films, and the spiced pepparkakor that I love to eat with cheese. Christmas in the Cotswolds was the best possible representation of my late surrogate mum Ingela – her warmth, energy, humour and generosity becoming even more evident at this time of year. Without her, we've been faced with reshaping the rituals into something new. But I am confident I'll still be making pepparkakor for many years to come.

Beetroot gravadlax, cucumber pickle, horseradish sauce

Gravadlax always makes an appearance on the Christmas Eve smörgåsbord. You can buy it from the supermarket, but it's never quite as lovely as it is made from scratch. The stunning pink of the beetroot and the botanical warmth of the gin give this recipe a festive flair. It is lovely for midsummer too, but in deep winter, when it's dark not long after three, it provides some colour on the table on Christmas Eve.

Makes enough for 12

1. If you have a dish that the salmon will fit into lengthways, then leave it whole. If not, slice it in half through the middle, and place the two pieces side by side in a dish (lined with parchment paper if the fillet is without skin). It's important that the salmon lies flat, and skin-side down.

2. Finely chop the beetroot (I'm lazy, and blitz them in a small food processor), and add the juniper, lemon zest, dill, salt and sugar. Pour in the gin. Pack this onto the salmon, ensuring it is entirely covered. Cover with plastic wrap and store in the fridge for between 24 and 48 hours (the longer you leave it, the more the salmon will be cured).

3. On the day you plan to eat the salmon, prepare the cucumbers. Slice them into long, thin ribbons with a vegetable peeler, and place in a bowl. Sprinkle over the salt and leave for an hour, to leach out some of the water. Bring the vinegar, sugar and coriander seeds to a simmer in a saucepan. Leave the mixture to sit for a couple of minutes to cool slightly, while you squeeze out the cucumber and then rinse it in some cold water. Pour the vinegar over the cucumber. Place in the fridge until chilled, then add the dill fronds.

4. To make the horseradish sauce, mix the horseradish, yoghurt, and lemon juice together. Season with plenty of pepper.

5. Scrape the cure off the salmon, and then rinse the last of it off with a little splash of cold water. Slice the salmon very

GRAVADLAX
1kg/2lb 4oz side of salmon, skin-on
3 raw beetroot/beets, scrubbed
6 juniper berries, crushed
Zest of 1 lemon
5 sprigs dill, chopped
100g/½ cup rock salt
50g/¼ cup demerara sugar
100ml/scant ½ cup gin

PICKLED CUCUMBER
2 cucumbers
2tbsp rock salt
100ml/scant ½ cup white wine vinegar
2tbsp granulated sugar
1tbsp coriander seeds
Fronds from 5 stalks of dill

HORSERADISH SAUCE
3tbsp grated horseradish (from a jar, or from the root)
100g/scant ½ cup yoghurt
Juice of 2 lemons
Black pepper

thinly, at an angle, starting at the thin tail end, and working your way up. Give yourself time to do this, as it does take a while and you don't want to be stressed or rushed once you have guests. Once sliced, it will keep, covered, in the fridge, for the next couple of days.

6. Serve the sliced salmon with a bowl of the pickled cucumber, the horseradish sauce, and some extra wedges of lemon.

Swedish meatballs

Ingela was never without a bag of homemade Swedish meatballs in the freezer. We eat a big dish of them every Christmas Eve, but they're welcome at any point: as soon as the temperature drops, I start to crave them. We often eat them with just lingonberry jam and boiled potatoes, but at Christmas it's worth making this creamy sauce, and a sharp winter salad to sit alongside.

Serves 6

1. First, make the meatballs. Put all the ingredients, except the oil, in a large mixing bowl. Squash together using your hands until well combined, and then roll generous teaspoons of the mixture into balls.

2. Pour the oil into a frying pan, and warm over a low heat. Fry the meatballs until golden all over, and cooked through – do break one open to make sure.*

3. While the meatballs are frying, make a start on the sauce. Melt the butter in a saucepan, and stir the flour into it with a wooden spoon. Cook for a couple of minutes. Pour the beef stock in slowly, and whisk until it starts to thicken. Season with Worcestershire sauce, Dijon mustard, soya sauce, salt, and pepper. Taste to make sure you're happy, then add the cream, whisk, and remove from the heat.

4. To make the salad, trim the base off the chicory and rinse the leaves. Core the apples, and slice into thin wedges. Toss these together, and crumble the Roquefort over the top.

5. Whisk the vinegar, mustard, and oil together, then season with salt and pepper. Toss through the salad, then top with the walnuts and parsley.

6. Serve the meatballs with a generous ladleful of the sauce, the salad, boiled potatoes and some lingonberry jam.

* You can refridgerate or freeze them at this point and re-heat when needed.

MEATBALLS
300g/10oz minced/ground beef
200g/7oz minced/ground pork
60g/1 cup soft white breadcrumbs
1tbsp chopped parsley
1tsp ground allspice
½tsp ground nutmeg
1 brown onion, finely diced
2 cloves garlic, minced
1 egg
Salt and white pepper
50ml/3½tbsp vegetable oil

SAUCE
30g/2tbsp butter
30g/3⅔tbsp plain/all-purpose flour
300ml/1¼ cups beef stock
1tbsp Worcestershire sauce
1tsp Dijon mustard
2tsp soya sauce
Salt and white pepper
100ml/scant ½ cup double/heavy cream

SALAD
4 heads chicory/endive
2 crisp eating apples
100g/3½oz Roquefort
1tsp cider vinegar
1tsp Dijon mustard
1tbsp olive oil
Salt and black pepper
50g/⅓ cup walnuts, toasted and chopped
20g/1 cup parsley leaves

As the days grow short

285

Pepparkakor

50ml/3½tbsp water
2tbsp golden syrup
80g/heaped ⅓ cup light brown sugar
20g/1½tbsp dark brown sugar
1tsp ground ginger
1tsp ground cinnamon
A pinch of ground cloves
75g/ ⅓ cup unsalted butter, cubed
1tsp bicarbonate of soda/baking soda
220g/1⅔ cups plain/all-purpose flour

If there are better Christmas biscuits, I have yet to find them. These work perfectly with cheese, or as a sweet bite with coffee. If there are a few of you about, you'll make your way through a batch remarkably quickly. They're Pippi Longstocking's biscuits – every time I make them, I picture her rolling out her dough on the floor, and then answering the door to Tommy and Annika, covered head to toe in flour.

Makes at least 60

1. Bring the water, golden syrup, sugars and spices to the boil over a low heat. Put the butter in a mixing bowl, and pour over the spiced syrup. Leave for a few minutes, until the butter has melted.

2. Sieve in the bicarbonate of soda and flour. Stir to combine and bring together into a dough. Leave the bowl in the fridge for at least an hour, or overnight, if you have time.

3. Preheat the oven to 200C fan/425F/gas 7. Flour your work surface, and roll out the dough as thinly as you can – 2mm/¹⁄₁₆in thick is about right. Line a couple of baking sheets with parchment paper. Cut hearts or stars out of the dough, or use the rim of a glass to cut circles if you prefer. Arrange them on the sheet, leaving a little space for them to spread slightly. A palette knife or flat knife will help you pick the biscuits up once you've cut them out. This dough is incredibly forgiving, so you can roll and re-roll as often as you need.

4. Bake in batches for 5 minutes, until slightly crisp around the edges. Leave to cool on the sheet for 5 minutes, and then completely on a wire rack. Serve plain or with cheese – they're lovely with Swedish cheese, a good Cheddar, or Stilton.

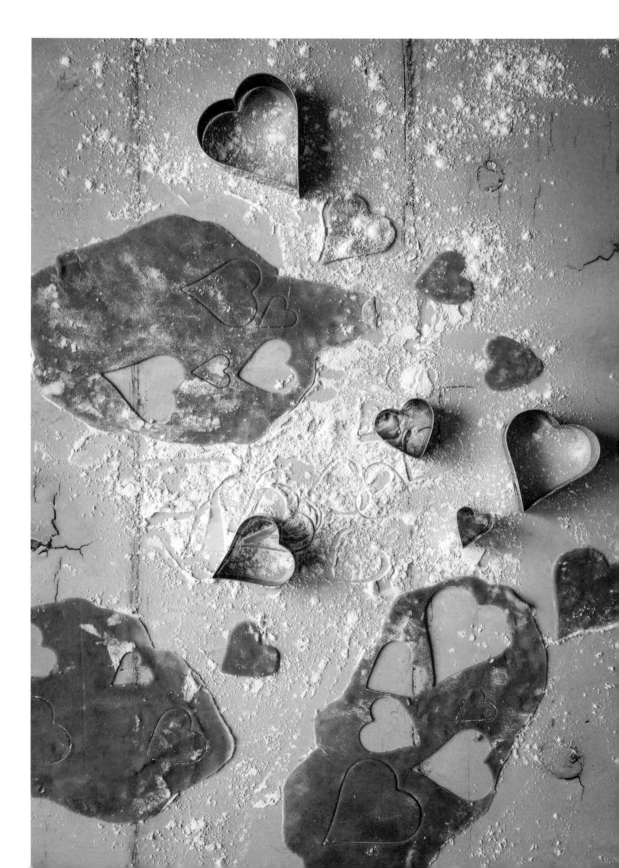

A fancy dinner to warm the soul

She wanted, she said, to cook a French dinner, a real French dinner, for this one time. Martine and Philippa looked at each other. They did not like the idea; they felt that they did not know what it might imply. But the very strangeness of the request disarmed them. They had no arguments wherewith to meet the proposition of cooking a real French dinner.

Babette's Feast, Isak Dinesen

When I turned thirty, I hosted a dinner I'd been talking about since I was in my early twenties; I wanted to recreate Babette's feast. Babette is a Parisian chef who arrives in the Norwegian town of Berlevåg as a refugee, and is taken in by two Protestant sisters. She moves in with them as their cook, and when, years later, she wins the French lottery, she spends all her winnings on a single, spectacular meal to say thank you. She prepares turtle soup, Blinis Demidoff, and Cailles en Sarcophage, and serves Veuve Cliquot, Amontillado sherry, Sauternes, and cognac. It is a meal that changes her guests – an experience they will think about for years to come.

The menu in the book is beyond extravagant, in both ingredients and in time spent in the kitchen. To do it in its entirety now is impossible – turtle and ortolan are completely off the menu (my wallet would have prohibited them even if the law hadn't) – so this is my, very much bastardized, version. It is still the most special meal I have cooked, but is achievable in a domestic kitchen, without a team of staff to help you.

New Year's Eve has never been my favourite night of the year; it's a reliably damp squib, in my experience. My inclination on a cold, dark night on the cusp of January is to be indoors, with good friends, food, and a bottle of wine. So my New Year's Eve suggestion to you, at the end of this book, is to avoid heading into town like the plague, and invite everyone to yours instead, for bird pies, blinis and Marsala cake. Play games and sing songs, and talk about all the brilliant things on the horizon for the coming year. As an added bonus, you won't have to battle with finding a cab or a night bus to take you home. I can't imagine a better send-off to the year, or a more appropriate way to welcome in the next one.

Blinis Demidoff

Ideally, it would be lovely to have a platter of these ready to hand around just after your guests arrive, but don't panic if you get distracted with table setting or organizing wine – enlist help from the early birds and flip blinis in the company of some pals. These are great with caviar, or roe, or with some smoked salmon. Make sure they're warm rather than hot when you serve them, or else the sour cream will melt right off.

Enough for 8

1. Whisk together the flours, salt and sugar in a mixing bowl. Warm the milk to body temperature in a saucepan, then stir in the yeast until it dissolves. Whisk in the sour cream, and the egg yolk.

2. Pour the liquid ingredients into the flour and whisk thoroughly. Cover the bowl with a tea towel and put it in a draught-free place to rise for an hour. It will almost double in size.

3. After an hour, beat the egg whites to stiff peaks, and then fold them into the frothy mixture. Cover with the tea towel again and leave for another hour. The mixture should be very light and full of bubbles – almost like a foam.

4. Once the batter has risen, warm half a tablespoon of the butter in a frying pan. Without stirring the mixture (you want to retain those bubbles), drop teaspoons of the batter into the pan. When the top of a blini is covered with bubbles, flip it over. Cook the blinis in batches until all the batter is used up.

5. Serve each blini warm, with a dollop of sour cream and a little spoonful of roe or caviar. They can be warmed through in the oven, but are best fresh, if you can serve them straight away. It's New Year's Eve; so pop open a bottle of champagne and enjoy.

BLINIS
60g/⅓ cup buckwheat flour
60g/⅓ cup strong white bread flour
A pinch of salt
A pinch of sugar
100ml/scant ½ cup milk
10g/2tsp fresh yeast (or 3g/1tsp easy-action yeast)*
75g/5tbsp sour cream
1 egg yolk
2 egg whites
30g/2tbsp butter

TO SERVE
50g/3½tbsp sour cream
Caviar or fish eggs

* I love the flavour of fresh yeast here, and am lucky enough to be able to buy it at the supermarket. If you can't get your hands on any, easy-action yeast will work well too.

Individual bird pies with leeks and pâté

In *Babette's Feast*, she serves ortolan in pastry for the main course. A French delicacy, ortolan are tiny songbirds that were drowned in Armagnac and eaten whole. It is a practice which is now (rightly) outlawed, but the bird, pastry, and Armagnac combination is still delicious. Though this recipe may seem lengthy, none of the steps are particularly difficult, and much of the work can be done in advance. It is a properly fancy centrepiece and looks really special on the table, so save it for an important occasion.

Serves 8

1. First, make the pâté. Bring a tablespoon of the butter to a foaming heat in a frying pan and fry the shallot for a couple of minutes until soft. Add the livers and thyme, and cook for a couple of minutes until the livers are browned on all sides, but still a little pink in the centre – cut one open to check.

2. Spoon everything into a food processor, but keep the frying pan on the heat. Add the Armagnac to the pan and cook off for a couple of minutes. Turn off the heat.

3. Blitz the livers to a smooth paste. Pour in the Armagnac, cream, salt, pepper, and allspice. Cube the rest of the butter and, with the food processor running on low, drop it in piece by piece. Pour the pâté into a container and transfer to the fridge for an hour to set. This can be done a day or two in advance, just make sure you don't eat the lot on toast before you get to the pies.

4. To prepare the leeks, peel them of their outermost layers, and give them a good rinse under cold water. Preheat the oven to 180C fan/400F/gas 6. Slice the leeks into thumb-sized pieces and place in a roasting tray. Season with the thyme, oil, and salt. Roast for 30 minutes until tender.

5. Meanwhile, make the sauce. Rehydrate the porcini mushrooms in 75ml/5tbsp boiling water. Melt the butter

PÂTÉ
45g/3tbsp butter
1 shallot, finely chopped
125g/4½oz cleaned chicken livers, diced
½tsp chopped thyme
2tbsp Armagnac
1tbsp double/heavy cream
A pinch of salt
Black pepper
1tsp ground allspice

LEEKS
3 leeks
1tbsp thyme leaves
2tbsp olive oil
A pinch of salt

SAUCE
20g/scant 1 cup dried porcini mushrooms
1tbsp butter
3 shallots, sliced
2 cloves garlic, minced
60g/1 cup chestnut/ cremini mushrooms, diced
1tbsp plain/all-purpose flour
3tbsp Armagnac
200ml/generous ¾ cup chicken stock
Black pepper

CHICKEN
2tbsp butter
6 chicken thighs, boned, with skins on

PIES
1kg/2lb 4oz ready-made puff pastry
2 eggs

in a small saucepan, and add the sliced shallots. Fry for a couple of minutes, then add the garlic and cook until fragrant. Dice the rehydrated mushrooms and add to the pan, along with the fresh mushrooms. Cook until golden brown. Sprinkle the flour over them, and then stir. Pour in the Armagnac, and simmer away for a couple of minutes. Add the stock, and cook until thick. Season with plenty of pepper and turn off the heat.

6. To prepare the chicken, warm the butter in a large frying pan. Fry the chicken skin-side down until crisp and golden, and then flip over until cooked through.

7. Finally, make the pastry shells. Roll out two-thirds of the puff pastry to 5mm/½in thick, and cut out 16 discs, 12cm/4½in. Place them on a couple of lined baking sheets. Beat the eggs, and paint the top of each disc with the egg wash.

8. Roll out the final third of the pastry, again to 5mm/½in thick, and cut 8 more 12cm/4½in discs. Make a cut inside them with a smaller glass or biscuit cutter, and discard the inside circle. Place the hollow circle on top of 8 of the discs, so that it forms a border. You're essentially making large vol-au-vent cases: 8 rimmed bases and 8 lids. Paint the circles in egg wash, ensuring not to paint the sides, or they'll struggle to rise.

9. Once the leeks are out of the oven, increase the temperature to 200C fan/425F/gas 7, and put the pastry cases and lids in. Bake until risen and golden brown; this should take 15–20 minutes.

10. While the pastry bakes, make sure the leeks are kept warm, re-heat the sauce, and slice the hot chicken thighs into strips.

11. Place the pastry shells on individual plates, push the pastry in the middle down so you have a well, and spread a tablespoon of pâté onto the base. Add a couple of lengths of leek, then distribute the chicken between the pies. Place a pastry lid on top. Bring the sauce hot to the table, and allow people to add their own.

Marsala cake with roasted fruit

CAKE

450g/3¼ cups strong white bread flour
10g/2tsp salt
15g/4tsp easy-action yeast
75g/⅓ cup caster/superfine sugar
160ml/⅔ cup milk
4 eggs
200g/¾ cup + 2tbsp butter, softened

SYRUP

200g/1 cup caster/superfine sugar
100ml/scant ½ cup Marsala

ROASTED FRUIT

150g/5½oz fresh figs
300g/10oz red grapes
150g/½ cup honey

WITH

60g/½ cup icing/confectioner's sugar
300ml/1¼ cups double cream
1tsp vanilla bean paste, or seeds from a vanilla pod/bean

EQUIPMENT

A large bundt tin/pan

In Isak Dinesen's novella, the guests finish the meal with pudding wine, and a plate of grapes, figs, and peaches. But in the film version, a cake appears: a booze-soaked savarin with fruit and cream. It's a rich dessert, so I'd leave your guests a good hour or so between the bird pie main and this, but it is New Year's Eve. There's a lot of evening to fill. Bringing this out at midnight, with a toast to the New Year, would be perfect. The cake can be made the day before, and kept covered somewhere cool. Warm the fruit through before you serve, and whip the cream at the final moment.

Serves 8

1. Pour the flour into a large mixing bowl, and add the salt on one side and the yeast and sugar on the other. Warm the milk to body temperature in a saucepan, and then whisk the eggs into it. Pour over the flour, and bring together with your hands into a dough.

2. If you have one, this next step can de done in a mixer with a dough hook. Knead the dough until soft and elastic; it will take about 5 minutes in a mixer, or around 10 minutes by hand. Start to add the butter in pieces, ensuring that each bit is incorporated before you add the next. Once the butter has all been incorporated, put the dough into a bowl, cover, and leave to rise for an hour or so in a warm place. It should double in size.

3. Once the dough has risen, grease a bundt tin and dust the sides and base with sugar to ensure the finished cake comes out easily. Pour or pipe the dough in, manoeuvring it around so that it is evenly distributed. Cover, and leave to increase in size again by one and a half times; the dough should not quite reach the top of the tin.

4. Preheat the oven to 160C fan/350G/gas 4. Once the dough has risen, transfer the tin to the oven, and bake for 50 minutes to 1 hour. It should be well risen and golden brown, and a skewer inserted into it should come out clean.

5. Remove from the oven and, while still warm, invert the tin and allow the cake to fall onto a cooling rack. If necessary, you can guide a flat knife around the edges to loosen it first. Gently place the cake on a dish or plate with a lip; something that can hold liquid.

6. To make the syrup, warm the sugar and Marsala in a saucepan, until the sugar dissolves. Slowly pour a third of it over the cake, allowing it to soak in and then collect around the bottom. Pour over another third, wait again, and then pour the final third over the cake. Allow it to stand for an hour, and then wrap it carefully in plastic wrap and transfer to the fridge overnight if you're making it in advance.

7. To prepare the fruit, line a roasting tray with parchment paper and turn the oven to 200C fan/425F/gas 7. Halve the figs, but leave the grapes whole, and arrange them in one layer in the tray. Drizzle over the honey, and roast for 30 minutes until caramelised.

8. When you're ready to serve, sieve the icing sugar into the cream, and whip it to soft peaks. Whisk through the vanilla. Serve slices of the cake with a spoonful of the warm fruit, and the cream.

As Christmas approaches I turn to these old favourites...

Stay inside to avoid the clatter and rumble of Bonfire Night, and stir up the Christmas pudding with *My Naughty Little Sister*. Take Amabelle Fortescue up on the offer of a bedroom in Mulberrie Farm, and visit the neighbours for a slice of *Christmas Pudding*. Drink a cup of Christmas punch at Miss Greythorne's with Will and his siblings, despite the knowledge that (elsewhere) *The Dark is Rising*. Discover *How Winston Delivered Christmas* and treat it as your very own advent calendar. Join Laura Morland, and all her endlessly diverting neighbours, in *High Rising*. Come round for *An Almost Perfect Christmas* with Nina and her family. Sit down to a feast with the Whos, young and old, and attempt to work out *How the Grinch Stole Christmas!* Join *The Jolly Christmas Postman* on his rounds through the village. Spend Thanksgiving with Meg and Calvin in *A Swiftly Tilting Planet*. Thrust open *The Box of Delights* on a dark, wintry night. Head off on an adventure with Bonnie and Sylvia as they're pursued by *The Wolves of Willoughby Chase*. Greet *A Christmas Carol*'s Ghosts of Christmas Past, Present, and Future, as they pay their visits to Ebenezer Scrooge. Make time for reading *The Night Before Christmas* on Christmas Eve, and go off to bed with a head full of sugarplums, and the sound of reindeers' hooves on the roof. Decorate *The Fir Tree* with the Moomins, and drink a cup of delicious eggnog.

Recipe index

Reading index

Y

Bibliography

In writing this book, I am indebted to many other cooks – ones I have stood in a kitchen with, and ones I have never met but whose recipes I have made and re-made over the years. Where I am clear of the origin of a dish, I have tried to credit it in the introduction to the recipe itself. However, there are so many recipes that have found their way into my repertoire whose origins are less clear: I have forgotten whether they came from my mum (or, through her, from one of the cookbooks on her shelves), from an article I happened across, or from a book that sits in my kitchen now. After years of cooking these dishes from memory and from instinct, their sources can be tricky to trace. I feel it is only right, therefore, that I point you in the direction of the books and people who taught me to cook, and to whom I continue to turn:

Stephanie Alexander's *A Cook's Companion*, an encyclopaedic tome, which provides invaluable information on almost every ingredient you can imagine.

Julia Child's *Mastering the Art of French Cooking*, which coached me through all manner of French sauces, and regional French cuisine.

Felicity Cloake's perfect 'How to cook the perfect...' column in the *Guardian*, is where I often find myself when looking into the history of a dish, and all those who have cooked it before.

Anna Del Conte's *Gastronomy of Italy* and *Portrait of Pasta*, which I read cover-to-cover in my cold London flat one winter, and which made me want to master pasta (and move to Italy).

Jane Grigson's *Fruit Book* (all her books are wonderful, but this is my favourite and the one I refer to the most).

Diana Henry's entire oeuvre (though especially *Food from Plenty*, *A Change of Appetite*, and *How to Eat a Peach*) is a constant inspiration for the food I cook and eat.

Nigella Lawson's *How to Eat*, and everything she has written since; books that have been my roadmap for cooking and for entertaining since I was twelve years old.

Dan Lepard's *Short and Sweet*, which is full of wonderfully dependable recipes for baked goods – particularly pastry.

Samin Nosrat's *Salt, Fat, Acid, Heat*, which provides clarity, reassurance, and scientific certainty, alongside warmth, and enthusiastic support.

Claudia Roden's *The Food of Italy*, for the culinary information on Liguria.

Niki Segnit's *The Flavour Thesaurus*, to which I turn with extraordinary regularity.

Nigel Slater's *Tender Vol 1* and *Tender Vol 2*, which I regularly pull off the shelf for seasonal inspiration. And *Kitchen Diaries*, which I spent years using as a 'What Would Nigel (and, therefore, should I) Eat Today?' guide.

Yukari, who taught me about Japanese seasoning, flavouring, and techniques in her Tokyo kitchen (her classes are available to book on Airbnb experiences, and are a true joy).

And... countless YouTube videos which helped me work out how to fold char siu bao so they remain closed while they steam.

Thank you

To my family – Mum, Dad, Geoff, Cheryl, Luce, and Justin – for the constant inspiration, generosity, and love. I wrote a second book so that you'd all have to come back for another launch party. Can't wait to see you soon.

To my other family – Chris, Anna, Tom, and Mia – for your endless support and enthusiasm, and for being the most extraordinary family I could have been adopted into. I feel enormously lucky to have all of you in my life.

To Tom: housemate, dear pal, and inventor of the Tom Jacob Special. For the weekend I made you eat four crème brûlées, for ordering pizza or making school dinners when I couldn't be bothered to cook, for a thousand cups of tea, and for your love, and the countless words of support.

To Liv, best of (kitchen) wives, and best of women, for every (long) hour we've spent standing at a hob together. So many recipes here are better because of you. I am better for knowing you.

To Maddy, for your vision, your support, your reassurance, and for taking such wonderful care in bringing the book to life. I'm so lucky to work with you.

To Zoe, for your guidance, your care, and your enthusiasm – and for being a brilliant agent from the very beginning.

To Lean, for your superlative photos, your kindness, your patience while I bluster about, and your artistry in putting everything together. I can't believe I get to work with you doing this – it's such an unending joy.

To Anna, Nicola, and Granny, for the use of your beautiful homes while we cooked and photographed all this food. And to the residents of Viridian Retirement Village, for your ovens, and the gardens, and for making sure we didn't have any leftovers.

To Bry, for quietly putting the set-up for the endpapers together, and doing such a truly extraordinary job.

To Mum, Bry, Granny, Nicola, Bex, Jess, and Geoff, for running to the shops for ingredients and props, for helping us stage photographs, for recreating my recipes with such love and care, and for making the whole book possible.

To Katya, Bex, Ben, Nic, Zoe, and Max, for your beautiful hands.

To Ella, for your endless reassurance and championing, and for heading out to fetch various types of sugar in order to test the brownies.

To everyone on Spillman's (most especially Misha, Mackie, Max, Tilly, Kim, Nina, and Rosa), for helping me eat all the test recipes, and providing enormously valuable feedback.

To the aunts, for being the best cheer squad.

To every bookseller and librarian who supported the first book so enthusiastically, and who pressed it into the hands of so many readers. There are too many of you to name individually, but special mention must be made to Rosie at Waterstones, who not only organised multiple brilliant events (and suppers), but who has become a real pal beyond the bookshelves.

To everyone at Head of Zeus, who has supported and championed me, and the books, from the outset. I apologize wholeheartedly that I no longer live in London and never bring cake in anymore.

To Jessie, for your gorgeous design and glorious enthusiasm.

To everyone who bought the first book, who gave it to a friend, who borrowed it from the library, who cooked from the blog, who read my work in the *Guardian*, who found me somewhere else online. It's impossible to convey to you just how much your support means.

Finally, and most of all, to Ingela. For your love, your support, and your continuing presence in the kitchen. For every Christmas, every wild garlic season, every crayfish party, and every midsommar. Your influence on this book is immeasurable.

Extended copyright